Clipper Studies in the American Theatre
ISSN 0748-237X
Volume Three

The Italian Theatre in San Francisco

*Being
A History of the Italian-Language Operatic,
Dramatic, and Comedic Productions
Presented in the San Francisco Bay Area
Through the Depression Era,
With Reminiscences of the Leading
Players and Impresarios of the Times*

**Compiled by
Lawrence Estavan**
Edited by Mary A. Burgess

R. REGINALD
The Borgo Press
San Bernardino, California □ MCMXCI

THE BORGO PRESS
Publishers Since 1975
Post Office Box 2845
San Bernardino, CA 92406
United States of America

* * * * * * * *

Copyright © 1991 by Mary A. Burgess.

All rights reserved.
No part of this book may be reproduced in any
form without the expressed written consent of the publisher. Printed in the United States of America by Van
Volumes Ltd. Cover design by Highpoint Type & Graphics.

Library of Congress Cataloging-in-Publication Data

Main entry under title:

The Italian theatre in San Francisco : being a history of the Italian-language operatic, dramatic, and comedic productions presented in the San Francisco Bay Area through the Depression Era, with reminiscences of the leading players and impresarios of the times / compiled by Lawrence Estavan ; edited by Mary A. Burgess.
  p. cm. — (Clipper studies in the American theatre, ISSN 0748-237X ; vol. 3)
Includes index.
ISBN 0-89370-364-8 : $22.95. — ISBN 0-89370-464-4 (pbk.) : $12.95
  1. Theater—California—San Francisco—History. 2. Italians—California—San Francisco—History. 3. San Francisco (Calif.)—Popular culture—History. I. Estavan, Lawrence. II. Series: San Francisco theatre research. III. Series.
PN2277.S4I8 1991   87-869
792'.09794'61—dc19   CIP

FIRST REVISED EDITION

CONTENTS

Acknowledgments — 7

Introduction: Il Teatro Italiano, by Mary A. Burgess — 9

Chronology — 11

PART I. THE POPULAR THEATRE

1. The Origins of the Theatre — 15
2. The Italian Audience — 17
3. The Apollo Theatre — 18
4. The Signora Impresario — 19
5. A Calamitous Cavelleria Rusticana — 20
6. The Bersaglieri Hall — 21
7. The Circolo Famigliare Pisanelli — 22
8. An American at the Circolo Famigliare — 23
9. Programs with Verve and Variety — 26
10. Popularity of the Circolo — 28
11. The Italians' Technique in Acting — 29
12. The Signora Impresario in St. Louis — 30
13. "We Want Carmen": A Near Tragedy — 31
14. The Nickelodeons — 32
15. Stenterello Comes to San Francisco — 33
16. The Origin of Stenterello — 35
17. The Washington Square Theatre — 37
18. The Stenterellate — 39
19. Large and Varied Repertoires — 40
20. Shakespeare in North Beach — 41
21. The Maori Company — 42
22. The Popularity of Shakespeare — 43
23. The Maori Repertoire — 45
24. The Italian Theatre Inactive — 47
25. The Liberty Theatre — 48
26. Teresa de Matienzo and Alfred Aratoli — 49
27. The Return of Stenterello — 50
28. The Passion Play — 51
29. Carlo Tricoli — 52

30.	Blackstone vs. the "Boards"	53
31.	Stenterello Becomes Passé	54
32.	Farfariello Comes West	55
33.	The Farfariello Macchiete	56
34.	Farfariello: Ambassador from Little Italy	58
35.	The Career of Tina Modotti	60
36.	New Muses and a Calling	62
37.	"Two Bit" Opera	63
38.	"Sing for their Supper"	65
39.	The Mexican Invasion	66
40.	The Alessandro Eden Theatre	67
41.	The Genius of La Alessandro Again	68
42.	The Last of Stenterello	70
43.	The Minciottis	71
44.	The Schism	73

PART II. IL TEATRO ITALIANO

1.	The Italian Theatre	77
2.	Mimi Aguglia	79
3.	L'Aguglia and D'Annuzio	81
4.	European Triumphs	83
5.	L'Aguglia in America	84
6.	Second Week at the Cort	86
7.	At Washington Square	88
8.	Elenora Duse	89
9.	The Return of Mimi Aguglia	91
10.	The Aguglia Repertoire	93
11.	Genesis of the Teatro Italiano	95
12.	The Teatro Italiano at the Community Playhouse	96
13.	Goldoni and Pirandello	98
14.	The Teatro Italiano Carries On	99
15.	At the Greenroom Playhouse	101
16.	At the Golden Bough Playhouse	102
17.	Seragnoli and the Popular Theatre	104
18.	Conclusion	106

Notes 107

Bibliography 108

Appendix I: Mimi Aguglia 109

Appendix II: Repertoire of the Teatro Italiano 111

Indexes:

Actresses	113
Actors and Impresarios	114
Theatres, Halls, Playhouses	115
Companies and Troupes	116
Plays and Operas	116

ILLUSTRATIONS

1.	First Program of the Italian Theatre	6
2.	Signora Antonietta Pisanelli Alessandro	14
3.	Two Famous Stenterellos	38
4.	Carlo Tricoli	76
5.	Mimi Aguglia	97
6.	A Typical Fan Program	103
7.	Three Leading Actors of the Italian Theatre	120

*First Program of the Italian Theatre
in San Francisco: April 9, 1905*

ACKNOWLEDGMENTS

Under the auspices of the United States Works Progress Administration, Northern California District, San Francisco, in 1939, the following Project Editorial Staff produced *The Italian Theatre in San Francisco* as part of a larger, on-going research project. Their dedication and labors are hereby acknowledged:

Editor: Lawrence Estavan; Research Direction: Matthew Gately and Jack W. Wilson; Monograph Writers: George Ducasse, Harrison Fox, Alan Harrison, Hector Rella, and Eddie Shimano; Research Assistants: Gretchen Clark, Miguel Gomez, Michael Krepshaw, Dorothy Phillips, Edward Springer, and Eldridge Warner; Bibliography and Proofreading: Beatrice Frohlich, Anne Nichols, and Elleanore Staschen; Production: William Facey, Clara Mohr, William K. Noé, and Olive Walsh; Cover and Decorations: N.Y.A. Art Project under Franz Brandt's Direction; Original Cover by Dorothy Hansen; Original Decorations: Charlotte Hammill and Ethelda Mann; Photo Reproduction: M. H. McCarty. Although the entire research and stenographic staff on the project assisted in the preparation of this monograph at various stages in production, particular credit should be given to George Ducasse for his rewrite work on the entire monograph.

In addition, we are indebted to the following members of the Italian Colony, whose lively reminiscences, documented by scrapbooks, newspaper clippings, photographs, and other data, furnished the basis of the story of *The Italian Theatre in San Francisco*:

Signora Antonietta Pisanelli Alessandro, pioneer impresario, singer, actress, and chief support of the Italian theatre of San Francisco. She was a chief source of information on the early days of the theatre.

Argentina Ferraù and *Vladimiro Brunetti*, actor-directors of the Teatro Italiano. Theirs is the most intimate connection with the theatre; through them was obtained much of the information in this monograph—through interviews and the loan of scrapbooks containing programs and newspaper clippings.

Primo Brunetti, veteran actor in the Italian theatre. He supplied interesting information concerning the Italian Shakespeare performances, and the history and background of Stenterello.

Rino Lanzoni, in his double capacity as *metteur-en-scene* (Old Venice Shop, 521 Sutter Street) and organizer of Il Teatro Italiano, as well as his position as secretary of the Cenacolo Club. He was one of the theatre's most energetic supporters. From him came an account of the history, difficulties, and aims of the Teatro Italiano.

Ettore Patrizi, editor of *L'Italia*. He was the sponsor of Mimi Aguglia and her company, and was familiar with the early history of Il Teatro Italiano. He gave this project access to the files of his newspaper and lent copies of some of his writings on the history of the Italians in San Francisco—a necessary background for the study of the Italian theatre.

Camillo Porreca, veteran impresario of the Italian theatre and opera. Through his reminiscences and his extensive collection of photographs, programs, and clippings, much light was shed on the first Stenterello, the "Two-Bit" Opera, and Farfariello.

Ottorini Ronchi, critic and editor of the Italian daily, *La Voce del Popolo*. He furnished much of the background of the Italian theatre and the nature and origin of the Italian Colony, including such highlights as the remarkable career of Tina Modotti.

Esther Rossi, secretary of the Italy-America Society. As representative of one of the organizations sponsoring Il Teatro Italiano, she was an authority on the financial background of the institution. From her came information concerning the people who subscribed to and supported Il Teatro Italiano.

Oreste Seragnoli, chief source on the popular theatre movement.

Mario Scarpa, veteran actor of the Italian theatre, then with the Federal Theatre. Much of the material in this monograph was supplied through his scrapbooks and interviews.

Carlo Tricoli, an actor in the Italian theatre who eventually became assistant district attorney of San Francisco during the era in which this monograph was prepared.

INTRODUCTION
Il Teatro Italiano

This monograph was originally prepared by the Federal Writers Project of the Works Project Administration, a "make-work" government agency established by the Roosevelt administration to provide jobs for unemployed writers during the Depression Era. This particular project ambitiously attempted to record theatre history, especially of ethnic groups, as it had evolved in the city of San Francisco. Although at least half of the proposed volumes in the series were completed, all were poorly mimeographed and bound, and survive today only as tattered, yellowing volumes in a handful of American libraries. The present volume has been edited and reset in the hope that the information will be preserved for yet another generation.

Obvious anachronisms have been removed, and I have also corrected some minor problems with the chronology, moving several chapters to what appeared to be more logical and readable locations. For the most part, however, the textual material included herein is reproduced very closely to what was originally published. *The Italian Theatre in San Francisco* was based on the researchers' contemporaneous interviews with the subjects of this monograph, many of whom were still living and working in San Francisco at the time, and as such, represents a valuable oral record of the development of popular theatrical culture in one of the most European of American cities.

It should be noted that the theatre was heavily influenced by the personalities of those artists and impresarios who were responsible for its existence. Strong family units, some with deep roots in the Italian theatre of the old country, left an indelible mark on this unique art form. The story of the San Francisco theatre is inseparably linked with the personal histories of these remarkable individuals. Hopefully, some sense of the dedication and fire which breathed life into this ethnic theatre has been preserved here.

The material principally covers two eras, pre-World War I, and the period between the wars through 1938, the year of original publication. No obvious political overtones are noted, although several references to Mussolini appear towards the end of the volume. It can be assumed, however, that the onset of the German and Italian invasions which brought about the beginning of World War II, together with the eventual positioning of Italy amongst America's foes, wreaked havoc on attempts to preserve Italian culture on these shores, no matter how noble the motive.

No further research on the fate of the Italian theatre has been undertaken in connection with the re-publication of this volume. The sunset of our nation's last age of innocence which immediately preceded the onset of World War II would seem to be a natural cut-off point. The effects of the war on the Italian theatre and culture, as well as on the Italian community itself, and the continuing story of ethnic theatre in the San Francisco Bay Area, might well be the topic of another volume.

We will content ourselves for now with examining a far less-complicated era—the history and transformation of the Italian theatre in the city of San Francisco during the first forty years of the twentieth century.

—Mary A. Burgess
San Bernardino, California
January 18, 1991

CHRONOLOGY

1850-90	Strolling magician, Mr. Rossi, opens his Italian Theatre on September 12, 1850. Amateur shows by Italian societies. *La Sonnambula* performed 1853 on Coast. First newspaper established 1859.
1890	Mimi Aguglia born in Sicily circa 1890. *Compagnie filodrammatiche* (amateur companies) in San Francisco. The Apollo amateur theatre.
1903	D'Annunzio meets Aguglia as a child and is so impressed with her talent that he writes a play for her.
1904-06	Antonietta Pisanelli starts her professional theatre, Circolo Famigliare Pisanelli. The Rapone Company is the first professional Italian company to play in San Francisco. Aguglia marries Ferraù (1905).
1906	Stenterello comes to San Francisco.
1907-08	Establishment of the small variety houses: Iris, Beach, Bijou.
1909	Opening of Washington Square Theatre. The Cesare Company is established.
1910	Maori Company at Washington Square. Shakespeare is performed in North Beach. Compagnia Comica-Drammatica leaves the area; Stenterello and his troupe leave with them.
1910-12	Maori Company at Washington Square. Highest point ever reached by Italian Theatre in San Francisco. Aguglia pays first visit to San Francisco in March 1912.
1914	Mimi Aguglia plays in North Beach after touring the United States. Two weeks' engagement at the Cort Theatre followed by special performances for Italians August 3-9. Aguglia then tours Latin America. Her daughter, Argentina, is born in Buenos Aires.

1914-17	Theatre is quiescent in North Beach. Sporadic entertainment by different groups.
1917	Opening of Liberty Theatre. The Compagnia Città di Firenze of Alfredo Aratoli signals the return of Stenterello.
1917-18	Farfariello visits San Francisco at the Liberty.
1918	Farfariello leaves San Francisco to continue American triumphs. Bruno-Seragnoli Company at Washington Square.
1919	La Moderna Comic-Opera Company, La Moderna Grand Opera Company, and the Latin Quarter Opera Company are organized by Amelia Bruno. "Two Bit" Opera makes its appearance.
1924	Teatro Italiano de Varietà (Teatro Alessandro Eden) opened. Duse visits San Francisco.
1925	The last of Stenterello.
1925-28	Città de Firenze Company at Alessandro Eden. Minciotti Company at the Liberty. Two companies play in North Beach. The Schism.
1929	Puglia Company at Washington Square.
1931	Primo Brunetti, Bernardini, Seragnoli, and Scarpa form a company.
1932	Mimi Aguglia returns to San Francisco. At Washington Square (renamed the Milano), she establishes the Teatro Italiano and leaves North Beach.
1933	Mimi Aguglia returns to San Francisco at the Milano.
1933-34	Teatro Italiano is reborn in San Francisco.
1934	Milano season ends with *Fédora*, May 22.
1934-35	Teatro Italiano at the Community Playhouse.
1936-37	Teatro Italiano shifts to the Greenroom Playhouse.
1938	Teatro Italiano continues at the Golden Bough Playhouse. Seragnoli and his company carry on at the popular Italian Theatre.

PART I

THE POPULAR THEATRE

Signora Antonietta Pisanelli Alessandro

1. THE ORIGINS OF THE THEATRE

In September 1850, a strolling magician named Rossi rented the upper floor hall of a building on Kearny and Jackson Streets and attempted to establish himself in the highly competitive, lucrative and hazardous theatrical life of San Francisco. Signor Rossi opened his Italian Theatre on September 12 with a magic and ventriloquism act, dances by his wife, Fanny Manten, and songs and dances by Signorina Canova and Signor Suar. The public and critics were encouraging, crowding his performances and writing flattering notices. After four nights, however, the budding Italian Theatre burned to the ground.

Signor Rossi was a patient man. This was his fourth fire, but he did not give up. He reopened his Italian Theatre on Commercial Street between Kearny and Montgomery, in the building formerly occupied by Dr. Collyer's Model Artists. When his fifth fire occurred shortly afterward, however, Signor Rossi used his magic to a practical end. He made himself vanish completely out of San Francisco. When next heard of he was playing with his troupe in South America, making acrimonious remarks about the city by the Golden Gate.

Signor Rossi popped in and then out of the scene, scarcely making an impression upon the usually alert San Francisco consciousness. The newspapers during his brief stay here referred to him casually as "Señor" Rossi, obviously confusing him with a Spaniard. Indeed this probably happened to many Italians during the early days. There were thousands of French, Germans, and Mexicans, but only a handful of Italians—and these were lost in the crowd of their more numerous Latin cousins.

Throughout their earlier immigration the Italians were never very conspicuous. They were completely unlike the debonair adventurers from Paris. The first Italians to arrive in California were seamen and fishermen and laborers. In 1849 there were less than a hundred in the state. In 1852, however, there occurred a noteworthy cultural event in the history of the city. Giuseppe established a restaurant on an abandoned schooner, the *Tam O'Shanter*; and minestrone and cioppino arrived in San Francisco to stay.

Italian immigration, nevertheless, continued slowly. In 1859, when the Italians established their first newspaper in San Francisco, there were only about 300 who could be considered of Italian heritage within the city, with about 2,000 others scattered throughout the state. Not for many years was the flood of immigration released. By 1869 Italians began to trickle into California seeking a place in American life as farmers, laborers, fishermen and restauranteurs.

They came from all parts of Italy, delighted to discover a climate so similar to that of their homeland and eventually became among the most numerous of foreign populations here. These factors, among others, explain their persistence as a national group and the Italian quality of early North Beach. It was not until the late 1880s that the great wave from southwestern Europe began to sweep over America, reaching its crest in the post-war years, 1919-1922, just before the restriction of immigration. In 1890 the Italian colony numbered 5,212. By 1910 it had grown to 16,919. In 1938, at the time of this monograph's preparation, there were approximately 60,000 Italians in the North Beach Colony alone.

Italian colonies in America have been extraordinarily unified. The first immigrants came individually, then as families. Next whole villages and towns were transplanted to these shores. New York's Little Italy was strongly Southern: Neapolitan and Sicilian. North Beach had a different quality—the bulk of the population there was from Northern Italy, especially Tuscany. But there were also the Piedmontese, who ran the restaurants, the Genovese, and the Neapolitans and Sicilians, who worked out of Fisherman's Wharf. And it was the expansive Neapolitani who brought North Beach its theatre.

The Italian theatre got off to a late start, closely following the trend of immigration. Unlike their urbane French cousins who had preceded them, and who had brought their highly trained troupes with them, the Italians, who had been farmers at home, had generally come from small villages where the theatre was an unfamiliar institution. But Italy had a long tradition of the theatre and the theatre was possibly even more deeply rooted in Italian life than among the French. Every Italian immigrant could play the mandolin or guitar, sing operatic arias or folk songs, and every Italian loved to talk and to perform pantomimes. So there has always been an amateur theatre of sorts; and always an eager and enthusiastic audience.

As with the French, the theatre among the Italians was an important aspect of social life. An average American of the day went to the theatre only to be entertained; he sat quietly in his seat and applauded at the proper intervals; between the acts he smoked briefly or went outside for a quick drink. In the Latin theatre, however, there was not the hush and quiet; it was animated and gossipy. One came to look at the house and meet acquaintances; hence the *entr'actes* were very long and the theatre was never quite dark. In the Latin theatre the play was not the only thing. And the attitude of the Italian public, even more than the French, was simple and spontaneous; the theatre was an experience in which it participated energetically.

2. THE ITALIAN AUDIENCE

The theatre in time became the dominating social institution of the Italian colony. Because they were living in an alien land, the Italians were forced to isolate themselves from Americans; they were forced to become even more clannish than they had been in Italy. Then immigrants of the more educated and cultivated classes arrived: merchants, artists, and professional men. They too were unfamiliar with the new country and the new tongue and clung affectionately to their old language, their old traditions. In Italy they had been passionately addicted to the theatre; now they clamored for an Italian theatre in San Francisco that would be a living bond with the past, a renewal of their ties with the old world.

Before 1900 there had been Signor Rossi and other stray magicians, jugglers, acrobats and puppeteers from Italy who performed in circuses and vaudeville houses for American audiences. At a very early date Italian opera became a staple of the San Francisco theatre. Individual singers, like Biscaccianti and Tetrazzini were adored by the public. But the essentially Italian colonial theatre had its roots in the *compagnie filodrammatiche*.

The *compagnie filodrammatiche* were the beginnings of the popular theatre. These were the amateur groups of the various clubs and societies who put on sporadic performances before a charitable public. These performances were well-attended and there was plenty of material. All that was needed was a forceful and practical personality to weld all these elements together into a strong permanent theatre.

3. THE APOLLO THEATRE

On April 9, 1905 the Italian colony of San Francisco suddenly realized that such a personality had entered their midst. All week long large bills were being circulated everywhere in North Beach. On Fisherman's Wharf and in Washington Square groups congregated and discussed the exciting news. On Sunday evening, April 9, 1905, at the Teatro Apollo (formerly Apollo Hall where the clubs held their meetings and where the *compagnie filodrammatiche* gave their performaces) was given a *Grande Serata Straordinaria.* A varied program was offered in honor and benefit of the Neapolitan *canzonettista*, the Signora Antonietta Pisanelli. This was the first performance of the Italian theatre in San Francisco.

A rare program of this performance displays a dignified portrait of the esteemed Neapolitan singer, who was not only the beneficiary, but who did practically all the work. She sang several solo numbers and a group of duets with Signor Luigi, soprano, and G. Macagno. She played Santuzza in the dramatic one-act play by Giovanni Verga, *Cavalleria Rusticana,* which used music from Mascagni's opera. *Cavalleria Rusticana* was followed by a one-act farce entitled, *Prestami Tua Moglie per Dieci Minuti* (*Lend Me Your Wife for Ten Minutes*), which in turn was followed by a Grand Ball. Tickets for this great event were 25 cents and reserved seats were 50 cents.

4. THE SIGNORA IMPRESARIO

The career of the popular Italian theatre is closely identified with the career of Antonietta Pisanelli (later Alessandro) in San Francisco. She was indeed a remarkable personality. She united dark eyes, a pretty voice, and a vivacious manner, with shrewd business acumen. She won and lost several fortunes with her various enterprises, but never once did she lose her popularity with her compatriots—nor her astonishing vigor and resourcefulness.

In 1904 Antonietta Pisanelli came to California with her orphaned son. She had come to America as a child and, like most immigrants, had resorted to all kinds of expedients to earn a living. Early on she exploited her knowledge of Neapolitan folk songs, her verve and animation, and her fine stage presence. In 1895 there was no professional Italian theatre, even in New York, but there were the *societe filodrammatiche* and with one of these, the Società Fraterna at Giambelli Hall, the young woman made her debut. She became so popular at once that theatres everywhere seemed to spring up in her tracks. She sang, acted, and helped to organize four or five theatres in New York. Then her vast energy drove her to other cities. She played in Philadelphia, Chicago, New Haven, and in other industrial cities in Connecticut. A series of personal tragedies dogged her steps. In quick succession she lost her mother, her husband, and her youngest child. A desire to annihilate these memories in the new and distant land of California sent her across the country. She knew no one here and she was penniless, but her courage was unlimited, and she still could sing.

In San Francisco, Signora Pisanelli discovered, to her amazement, there were 16,000 Italians and not even one Italian theatre. She immediately took advantage of this situation. She rented the Apollo Hall for one night, rounded up all the available amateur actors, rapidly put them through their paces, and announced a varied program of songs and sketches. Standing room was sold out and Signora Pisanelli took in over $150. She had struck a bonanza.

For several nights there were Italian shows at the Teatro Apollo, eagerly crowded by her nostalgic countrymen. But the first professional theatre had not yet completely separated itself from the amateur theatre. There were still the unexpected disasters and the impromptu gaffs—which only enlivened the shows for the boisterous audiences. Settings were crude and liable to collapse or fall apart at any unlikely moment; so were the actors.

5. A CALAMITOUS CAVALLERIA RUSTICANA

A few days after its first performance, *Cavalleria Rusticana* was repeated. A new actor, an individual who in private life was a good barber, was carefully drilled in his part. It was a small but important role, that of the prologue, coming in at the beginning and explaining what had gone before. He acted also as a *point de depart* for the succeeding action. Signora Alessandro carefully impressed upon the debutant the importance of his role, and soon the curtain went up on the cardboard Italian countryside of *Cavalleria Rusticana*.

Santuzza, played by Signora Pisanelli, entered left, followed by Frank the Barber, who entered right. He had been elaborately made up, he wore a huge wig, long white whiskers and knee breeches several times too large for him. He came upon the stage pompously, turned about several times to display his brilliant presence before his numerous friends, strutted back and forth, and then opened his mouth to speak. The applause died down. Again Frank opened his mouth, but no words came out. He became suddenly aware that he had forgotten his lines. He looked about him in consternation. The prompter hissed his lines at him; from both wings they hissed his lines at him. Frank became confused. His head bobbed about in all directions. The audience also was trying to be helpful; everybody in the first three rows was hissing his lines at him. Gradually the barber-actor was overcome by a feeling of futility. His voice could not be distinctly heard over cross-currents of prompting. These were not the lines of the play; in fact Frank the Barber was so overwhelmed by emotion that he completely forgot his own language.

"Well, all right," he said, and, shrugging his shoulders despondently, walked off the stage.

Santuzza was left all alone on the stage, knowing her lines, but with no cues to respond to, and with nobody to address them to. But Signora Pisanelli's experience on the robust Italian stage had equipped her with many resources, and somehow the curtain that night fell on *Cavalleria Rusticana* before an audience hysterical with delight.

Signora Antonietta Pisanelli Alessandro, at the time of this writing, was a sparkling old lady of over 70 who had not yet lost any of her old-time fire and animation. At the recollection of that startling *Cavalleria Rusticana* she said: "Somehow we went through the play. I don't know how, but we did." She shook her head in wonderment at the recollection.

6. THE BERSAGLIERI HALL

As the Italian theatre become more substantial and permanent in San Francisco, these ludicrous misadventures became less frequent. Fumbling amateurs were replaced by smooth, well-trained actors. And Signora Alessandro brought to San Francisco the best Italian artists in America—among others, Maori, Farfariello, and Stenterello. Under her aegis the Italian theatre developed into the most lively and varied theatre in San Francisco.

Signora Pisanelli had not counted on the enormous popularity of her performances, crude though they were, at the Apollo Hall. She now had no doubts about the permanence of the Italian theatre in San Francisco. She promptly discovered a larger and more substantial building than the Apollo Hall, the Bersaglieri Hall on the corner of Stockton and Union Streets, and leased it for ten years. Now the Italian theatre was in full sway in San Francisco.

Every night Italian singers, musicians, dancers, and actors performed in the Bersaglieri Hall. Signorina Pisanelli wrote to New York to the famous Rapone Company and soon they were on their way across the continent. She wrote to the Cesare Company—and San Francisco began to blossom as the new center of the Italian theatre in America.

7. THE CIRCOLO FAMIGLIARE PISANELLI

North Beach welcomed this new institution; it crowded the Teatro Bersaglieri every night. Then came difficulties with the authorities. As a theatre, the Bersaglieri did not comply with fire department regulations and would have to be closed. Signora Pisanelli shrugged her expressive shoulders in resignation; the Teatro Bersaglieri was closed—and the next day it became the Circolo Famigliare Pisanelli, the Pisanelli Family Circle. Instead of rows of seats there were now little tables and chairs; but the stage was still there—it had become a *café-chantant*. On the stage the performers still sang, played musical instruments, and acted in dramas, comedies and farces. Now, of course, there were no admission charges, but the admiring public bought many drinks as the fascinating Signora went from table to table, exchanging greetings, and singing Neapolitan songs. North Beach enthusiastically welcomed the innovations; things were now even more sociable.

The astute Signora not only knew how to exploit her personality commercially, she also had all kinds of clever little schemes for making extra money. She rented the ground floor of the Bersaglieri Hall for various mercantile establishments. She sold advertising space on her programs and curtains. When customers complained of the heat she had paper fans manufactured and distributed them *gratis*—but both sides of the fans were covered with advertisements of barber shops, saloons, restaurants, furniture stores, and banks. When the customers complained of the cold she gave them the fans anyway.

8. AN AMERICAN AT THE CIRCOLO FAMIGLIARE

During 1905 and 1906 the Circolo Famigliare Pisanelli reigned supreme in North Beach, as a principal social institution—it was a combination of club, opera, theatre, and café. An elderly American gentleman, J. M. Scanland, visited the Circolo Famigliare Pisanelli often and became an authority on the subject of the Italian theatre. Writing in the *Overland Monthly* of April 1906 that he was impressed by the unusually high standards of performances at the Circolo, he said:

> Italians look upon opera as a necessity, and also strictly as an amusement, and they want it strong and good, artistically and musically. They care little for scenery—they want the acting, and upon this and the music everything depends. They do not like ranting or screaming, nor the posings of stage statues for effect. This unique Circolo makes little effort at scenic effects—the artists are expected to make their own scenes and pictures in dramatic acting. At times the little stage is well-crowded with characters, but there seems to be enough room for the most striking situations and dramatic scenes, and auditors are satisfied without the aid of scenery, which often covers the defects of bad acting.

The writer preludes a description of a typical performance at the Circolo by his very romantic impressions of Italian life:

> The patrons of the Famigliare Circolo arrive slowly, for in the quarter there is plenty of time for everything, and there is no need to be in a hurry when seeking amusement. About 8 o'clock, the floor of the Circolo is dotted with groups of different types—men with their families; others without families, young men with their senorinas (*sic*), and still others who have no senorinas, but may have some other young man's sweetheart tomorrow night. Gradually the circle is filled—perhaps there are six hundred in the two half circles—the two hundred in the gallery making themselves heard in the various dialects shouting "Let it go!" which is the same as "Heist de rag!" In the first circle there is a hubbub of voices and bursts of

> merry laughter. All are talking, each coterie in their own dialect. There are greetings of friends, smiles from lovers and mischievous glances from senorinas who are looking their sweetest in their costumes of various colors...

Scanland tries his best to gild the lily—to add a little color of his own. He continues:

> Suddenly the sweet, soft strains of "Heart Bowed Down," from *The Bohemian Girl*, or a gem from *Rigoletto* are heard. The hubbub ceases, and some who think they possess musical abilities accompany the orchestra by humming the chorus or whistling the air. The orchestration is very artistic, and when the music ceases there are shouts of admiration and an "*Echo!*" (*sic*).

But when Signora Pisanelli appears the old codger is transported. He uses much language to describe the star of the show, but with no other effect than to exhibit his amorousness:

> With the rise of the curtain Signorina (*sic*—Signora, unfortunately) Antonietta Pisanelli, the brightest star of the Circle, trips out upon the stage amid bursts of applause. She is prettily dressed in black, the dress cut décolleté, revealing shapely shoulders and the bust of a model. Her Neapolitan cameo face is stamped with intellectuality and refinement. Heavy brows arch her piercing velvety eyes—as black as midnight, yet flashing with the brightness of the diamond—the kind that drive men crazy. A profusion of coal black hair heightens the beauty of her classic face, which now changes from smiles to sadness as she sings of her lover who is not. That is, she wants one—a really nice lover. Her complaint is that all the senorinas (*sic*) have a lover and perhaps more, but she has not one. It would seem that upon one whom nature has showered so many gifts should have them by the score. Perhaps she desired an ideal that existed only in her imagination....

He continues in this sentimental vein for a time, getting more maudlin with every song. At length, after a lush description of *Funiculì Funiculà*:

> She answers the encore with "Love and Kisses." Her face is wreathed in smiles—the sadness has disappeared. She

has evidently found a lover who understands his business for she now tells all about love and kisses. It is a pretty, lively air, and is sung charmingly to make it piquant and spicy. During its rendition there are sighs of "Ah!" and "Ah-h-h!" and sounds of imitation kisses from some of the love-smitten gallants. As a finishing touch, to add fuel to the flame, she coquettishly places the tips of her fingers to her full-rounded lips, and with a delicate sibilant noise, tosses a kiss, fresh and warm, to the audience—catch it who can! Many echo the kiss each believing that he has caught it by wireless telegraph. A man high up in the gallery is evidently hit hard and expresses relief in an owl-like hoot, which creates uproarious laughter. But it is only a stage kiss and like the perfume of the rose, it is not for one—but for all....

9. PROGRAMS WITH VERVE AND VARIETY

Mr. Scanland's description of the Circolo is a little too subjective, a little too picturesque and romantic; and he appears to be too smitten by the charms of the bewitching Signora to resemble a sound critic. However, his prose does suggest the sponaneity and enthusiasm engendered by the completely popular quality of the performances, where all—actors, singers, audience—gaily participated.

"Gems from the Opera" were featured on the Circolo's programs. But even grand opera was padded for the exacting public. The opera was preceded by folk songs (called "love songs" by Scanland) and popular duets; and there were songs between the acts, completely irrelevant to the opera. On nights when tragedies or comedies were given instead of opera, the invariable farces, solos and duets were interspersed between the acts. One evening there would be Antonietta Pisanelli and Eleana Corta singing Neapolitan folk songs; there would be a comedy sketch entitled *The Music Lesson* with Signora Pisanelli and Signor Di Grazia; Signor and Signora Di Grazia would appear together in "a character sketch portraying provincial life, dressed in the quaint costumes of the district." And the reigning favorite, Signora Pisanelli, would appear last on the program to bring down a triumphant curtain.

Among the Neapolitan folk songs sung by Signora Pisanelli, none has become so popular in San Francisco as the rollicking "Funiculì-Funiculà." And yet very few who sing or hum or whistle it know that Naples owes its jolliest street song to the cable cars of San Francisco! For "Funiculì-Funiculà" is a paean to the funicular railway. The song was inspired by the exhilarating ascension of Mount Vesuvius in the Montesante tramway, built by the engineer Gagni after a visit to San Francisco. And then the song returned to San Francisco finding a cheerful accompaniment in the chirruping of the cables and the bumping, clattering rise and fall of the cars. Mr. Idwal Jones, who seems to be the first to have publicized the intimate relationship between the popular Neapolitan air and the San Francisco cable cars, takes pleasure in describing a crowd of Italian opera singers clinging to the straps and singing "Funiculì-Funiculà," boisterously unaware that they are riding in the first funicular railway in the world—and that their favorite song was conceived here.[1]

So the Signora Impresario performed a good service in cementing the lyrical Naples-San Francisco *entente*. She sang numerous Neapolitan songs, many of which were heard for the first time here. She dominated the stage of her little theatre. She exploited her popularity by always appearing last on the program (she also appeared first). The walls of her theatre displayed innumerable portraits of Signora Pisanelli with various expressions; there were large photographs of herself on her programs and on her fans. Her theatre was called the Circolo Famigliare Pisanelli. It was no miracle that her likeness was engraved on the minds of the inhabitants of North Beach and that her name was on everyone's tongue.

10. POPULARITY OF THE CIRCOLO

But Signora Pisanelli also gave her customers their money's worth. The repertoire of the Circolo Famigliare was long and varied. The Italian theatre was the only theatre which invariably changed its program nightly. A different opera every night was the rule at the Circolo Famigliare: one night there was music from *La Traviata*, next *Rigoletto*, on the next *Bohemian Girl*, then *Othello* and *Lucia di Lammermoor*. Then they skipped deftly to comedy, farce, tragedy, melodrama, burlesque—all spiced with popular songs. Also included in the repertoire was a peculiar Italian genre, the dialect comedy, whose effect depended almost entirely upon the locality where scenes were laid and the type of characters presented.

11. THE ITALIANS' TECHNIQUE IN ACTING

There was obviously no effort made at scenic effects. The actor himself created his own scene. The whole weight of the performance in the Italian theatre was on the acting, and the Italian tradition of improvisation, and of the Commedia dell'Arte, still flourished. The actor who must plunge into a different role every night cannot operate like a machine—as does the typical American performer who plays the same role night after night for months—or years. Such a phenomenon as personal acting—the actor always playing a variation of himself— could not possibly affect the Italian actor. He made rapid adjustments, every night entering into the spirit of a different character. For this reason he never memorized his lines. He had neither the time nor the patience; and he felt that a memorized role would cramp his style anyway. This was the tradition of the Commedia dell'Arte where the comedian improvised his part and where even a second performance of the same play was never quite the same. Because the Italian actor was generally extroverted and expressive, it was not difficult for him to enter into another character every night. He read the play once or twice, rehearsed a few times, grasped the spirit of the role, and was ready to perform. No embarrassing situations arose on the stage because the prompter was always there. The prompter was the most important prop of the Italian theatre. The gentle murmur of his voice accompanied the play like a constant anticipatory echo. Non-Italian audiences were often put off by the continuous sound of the prompter reading the entire play to the actors; for them the convention of the prompter could be as intolerable—or as quaint—as that of the property man in a Chinese play.

The Circolo Famigliare Pisanelli had all the ingredients of the popular Italian theatre; it had richness, variety, spontaneity, and vitality. The audiences filled the theatre with their enthusiasm; they contributed very little else. The actors received very little pay, but their playing was robust and impassioned and there was a breathless swing to the performances. Things went splendidly at the Circolo Famigliare Pisanelli.

12. THE SIGNORA IMPRESARIO IN ST. LOUIS

Then came 1906, the earthquake, and the fire. The desolate Rapone troupe contemplated the ashes of Circolo Famigliare Pisanelli, broke up into small companies, and toured the Pacific Coast. Some even went as far as the Eastern cities. They advertised themselves everywhere in large letters, *Superstitu de Terremoto San Francisco* (Survivors of the San Francisco Earthquake). They were received as heroes and martyrs by their sympathetic compatriots, and were a big success everywhere.

By 1907, when the smoke had cleared away, the Signora Impresario found herself again in San Francisco. But with seismographic intuition she had sold her theatre three days before the fire for the very profitable price of $20,000. She then had gone to St. Louis where the exposition was in progress and where great theatrical possibilities were offered. Having married again, she changed her name to Alessandro and handed over some of the minor managerial duties to her husband.

13. "WE WANT CARMEN": A NEAR TRAGEDY

St. Louis, however, turned out to be dangerous territory, and only Signora Alessandro's incredible resourcefulness averted a catastrophe. On arrival she hired a hall and had programs printed, announcing the popular one-act play, *Cavalleria Rusticana*, to be followed, as was the custom, by a Neapolitan folk song, "Carmè." There were the expected amateurish blunders, but somehow the play was finished and then the Signora, with a male member of the cast, appeared on the stage and sang the Neapolitan song. The curtain fell, the theatre lights went on, and the actors prepared to go home. But the audience did not want to go home: they were sitting very firmly in their dollar seats shouting: "We want *Carmen*! We want *Carmen*!" Signora Alessandro hurriedly scanned the program. Yes, it was there. The printer had made the obvious blunder, *Carmen* instead of "Carmè," and the audience was waiting for the four-act opera!

When it became evident to the audience that they were not going to get *Carmen*, that they were being defrauded by a lot of out-of-towners, they began to boil over with indignation. Italian audiences are tolerant, but they can also, at times, be most exacting. They shrieked "We want *Carmen*! We want *Carmen*!" But Signora Alessandro was equal to any emergency. She quickly slipped the box office receipts to her husband and said, "*Vatene Via!*" Next she pushed her little son onto the stage and urged, "*Canti!*" With the appearance of the small boy the audience (which was on the point of tearing the theatre apart and lynching the impresario) quieted down. Little Alessandro tremulously lifted his small voice and piped, "Wait Till the Sun Shines, Nelly." They applauded vociferously and he gave "In My Merry Oldsmobile." They yelled, "*Bravissimo, piccolino!*" and clamored for more. Then St. Louis was offered the incongruous spectacle of unhappy, brave little Alessandro singing favorite after favorite to furious applause, while Papa Alessandro scurried down dark alleyways clinging tightly to the cash. And for several months therafter the harmonious Alessandro family continued to triumph in St. Louis in the noblest traditions of the extemporaneous stage.

14. THE NICKELODEONS

By 1907 some of the other "survivors" had likewise found their way back to San Francisco and there was a recrudescence of the Italian theatre. One of these hardy and persistent pioneers was Mario Scarpa, a young man who had been introduced to the theatre under the auspices of the Signora Impresario disguised in blackface in *La Lupa del Mare* (*The Sea Wolf*). Scarpa joined Signora Alessandro now in opening one after another of a series of small houses. These impermanent theatres of the nickelodeon genre displayed, in addition to the primitive flickering moving pictures, Italian farces, vaudeville, and one-act sketches. Prices scarcely went above 5 or 10 cents. There was the Iris on Broadway, the Beach Theatre on the corner of Vallejo Street and Columbus Avenue, and the Bijou on the corner of Columbus Avenue and Stockton Street. These have long since become the sites of dignified mercantile establishments.

In negotiating for these theatres the Signora Impresario time and again revealed her indefatigable energy and astonishingly practical commercial sense. When she wished to construct the Beach Theatre an Irish priest at the St. Francis Church across the street proved obdurate. He had considerable influence, but Signora Alessandro found an Italian on the board of supervisors, a Mr. Calegari, and she got her license. The Signora could go far because she had the loyal Italian colony of San Francisco solidly behind her.

15. STENTERELLO COMES TO SAN FRANCISCO

The first Stenterello came to the tiny Bijou Theatre. Arturo Godi had occasionally played Stenterello at the Circolo Famigliare Pisanelli, but now, as a member of the company of Francesco de Cesare, this became his permanent role. With his usual enthusiastic inaccuracy, Scanland had thus described the Florentine *carattere* on his first appearances in this city:

> The Italians also have a keen sense of humor, and of the ludicrous. One of the farces very popular with the masses, is "Stenterello," which depicts a half-clown, half-comedian—the word "Stenterello" signifying a clown. (*sic*) The principal character takes the name of the play. He assumes several parts—at times he is a quack doctor, a servant, an umbrella mender, or a strolling player in the role of Hamlet. He is always hungry, like most barnstormers, has a craving for soup, and never seems to get his fill. His ambition is to marry rich, and in his hunt for a wealthy widow, in his various disguises, he is frequently mistaken for someone else who is being hunted, and consequently gets into trouble. The more he explores, the greater his trouble. Finally he is saved by his good luck and stupidity....Signor Godi is an excellent impersonator, and his entrance is always greeted with applause and laughter. Much of the success of this character depends upon the gestures and grimaces of the man in pursuit of soup and a wealthy widow...."[2]

At the Bijou, the Cesare Company produced a great variety of Stenterellate, besides a large repertoire of drama, opera, and farce. The little nickelodeon, with a capacity of only one or two hundred, could scarcely seat a fraction of the enormous numbers clamoring nightly for admission. With the advent of Stenterello, the Italian the-atre would never become more Italian—or more popular. For Stenter-ello was the people—the man-in-the-street of the city of Florence.

Stenterello was not usually the hero of the drama; he was simply a stock type, the projection of the common people who intrudes in every Florentine piece. We may picture a tense dramatic scene: the villain confronts the heroine, gnashing his teeth, while the heroine moans and wrings her hands. Passions are blazing. Emotions are at their peak. The audience is quivering on the edge of its seat. Then a grotesque figure comes sauntering out of the wings and walks nonchalantly upon the stage. The audience bursts into laughter. For this new character is eccentrically made-up and costumed: purple circles around his eyes, face streaked with red and white blotches; his hair hangs behind as a queu, the end curling up like a pig's tail; one of his front teeth is lacking. This bizarre creature is wearing a light blue jacket, a canary-yellow vest, black knee-breeches, fantastic picture stockings, and low shoes with large tin buckles. And perched impudently on the top of his head is an enormous three-cornered hat. It is the familiar Stenterello and the audience is hilarious. He points at the actors in the play, grimaces, makes a coarse comment, an indecorous gesture; the audience tumbles hysterically into the aisles.

For the past 150 years tradition says that every play produced in Florence must have Stenterello—every play, whether tragedy, melo-drama or farce. He is a purely local character, a stock type, a *carat-tere*, as differentiated from a *mashera* of direct Commedia dell'Arte origin. He is Stenterello, the simpleton, the emaciated country bump-kin, the gluttonous servant, the crafty fruit vendor, the shiftless drunkard, the menial with an heroic heart. He is the Florentine people.

Stenterello comes on the stage and goes off without the slightest regard for plot or action, making sly jokes in the Tuscan dialect on current events and personalities, burlesquing the characters in the play, playing the clown. Generally he speaks in the Tuscan dialect while the characters in the play speak pure Italian. Every region of Italy has its *carattere*; Naples has its Pulcinello who speaks Neapolitan, the Sicilians have their Pasquino, the Piedmontese their Gianduja, the Milanese their Menaghino, the Venetians their Zacometto. Because the majority of the Italian public of San Francisco were from Tuscany, they had only Stenterello.

16. THE ORIGIN OF STENTERELLO

Stenterello is a character created out of the Florentine common people, a crystallization of its vulgar, gay personality. He is a type, but not as immutable as the Commedia dell'Arte *maschera*. He is popular and variable; given, for example, to frequent changes of costume, although retaining the same traditional pattern throughout the ages. The first Stenterello was created in the 18th century by a popular actor of the Florentine theatre, one Luigi del Buono. The public synthesized the various roles played by its favorite actor and established the stock type, the thin, hungry man, Il Stento. Stenterello appeared later—an affectionate diminutive. The date of Stenterello's origin is suggested by his costume, which was a burlesque of the contemporary fashion. This costume which since has undergone minor variations was in opposition to the new costume introduced into Italy by the French.

Originally Stenterello had a small political function, anti-French, then anti-foreigner, in favor of Italian unity and independence. Later he became simply the man of the people, with a strong sense of justice, impulsively generous, protector of the weak and the helpless. His bold arrogance contrasts ludicrously with a persistent fidgeting anxiety; his language and gestures are frank and coarse. He gets his comic effects principally from grimaces, gestures, and pantomime. Because he has a special costume, although without a mask; because he has conventionalized characteristics and dialogue; because the actor who plays Stenterello generally plays nothing else and becomes identified with the part, Stenterello is, in reality, of the Commedia dell'Arte tradition; he is the permanent character transcending individual personalities.

The actor who plays Stenterello must merge himself into the character; he cannot play himself but must get his effects within the character, building it out, caricaturing it. He plays variations on the stylized theme, and it is here that the amazing expressiveness of the Italian actor comes into play; his body becomes plastically eloquent; he becomes a pantomimist. Stenterello was the darling of the masses. The instinct for pantomime today survives only among children and the common people; witness the popularity of Charlie Chaplin, who created a character in the Commedia dell'Arte tradition.

But today, even in Florence, the Stenterello tradition is dying out; plays are no longer rewritten for Stenterello. The public is becoming more sophisticated and Stenterello is considered too naive, like the circus clowns, something only for little children.

In San Francisco in 1907, however, Stenterello had his following; they crowded the little Bijou nightly to laugh at Godi with his clown make-up, his florid jacket, tight silk be-ribboned black breeches, his disparate socks and dainty slippers, playing the garrulous, fidgety, absent-minded Stenterello, slouching aggressively and incongruously into plays by Dumas, Shakespeare and Jules Verne. The little nickelodeons could no longer hold the enormous crowds of Italians in North Beach who flocked to laugh at and applaud their beloved Stenterello. A new, more spacious theatre was urgently needed.

17. THE WASHINGTON SQUARE THEATRE

Then the opportunity came; and as usual it was the brilliant fertile-brained Signora Alessandro who arranged for the opportunity. In 1909 there was a Russian church in Washington Square, on Powell Street between Union and Filbert Streets. In the heart of North Beach, it was the perfect site for an Italian theatre. All that was needed was enough cash or credit to buy the property and erect a theatre building—neither of which the Signora Impresario had at the moment. However, she had remarkable gifts, and she persuaded the influential politician, Abe Ruef, to supply the capital. The Washington Square Theatre was built, and when payment was not forthcoming from Signora Alessandro, it was rented to an American vaudeville company.

In North Beach this new enterprise was promptly enveloped by as much indifference as had submerged the Russian church. In a few months the discouraged American company moved out, abandoning the Washington Square Theatre to the joyful Italians. From then on it became the chief home of the Italian theatre in San Francisco. Here, in 1910, came the famous Maori Company from New York to play for two years in a brilliant repertoire that included everything from grand opera to Shakespearean tragedy; here, in 1914, Mimi Aguglia, the internationally celebrated tragedienne, played in North Beach, and again in 1932-34.

Here, between 1925 and 1928, Minciotti played, along with the second Stenterello, Alfredo Aratoli. Frank Puglia played here and Seragnoli; here, in 1919, Maestro Serantoni inaugurated the energetic era of the "two-bit" opera. Later, Washington Square went through the successive changes characteristic of the theatres of San Francisco. It became the Milano Theatre when it slipped out of the hands of the Italians and into a Jewish corporation; then it became an ultramodern, neon-lighted, streamlined cinema house called the Palace. And by 1938 the ghost of the Italian theatre flitted about in various halls and auditoriums, and in a tiny, though fashionable, extra-North Beach art theatre called the Golden Bough Playhouse.

But on April 10, 1909 the opening of the Washington Square Theatre as an Italian theatre was a great event. This was the first real theatre for the Italians, with a capacity of almost 1,000 seats. Cesare, the *capo comico* of the Compagnia Comica-Drammatica Italiana, announced exuberantly that the repertoire for the forthcoming season would include drama, comedy, farce, *bozzetti* (sketches), *romanze* (ballads), *pezzi d'opera* (operatic numbers), American songs and dances—with the brash and ubiquitous Stenterello, of course, intruding his inappropriate personality. Nor could the company be accused of indolence; the theatre would be open every day from 2 to 5 in the afternoon and from 6:30 to 11 in the evening. On Sunday the theatre would remain open from 1 to 11. And all this cornucopia would be emptied for nickelodeon prices—5 cents and 10 cents!

Two Famous Stenterellos

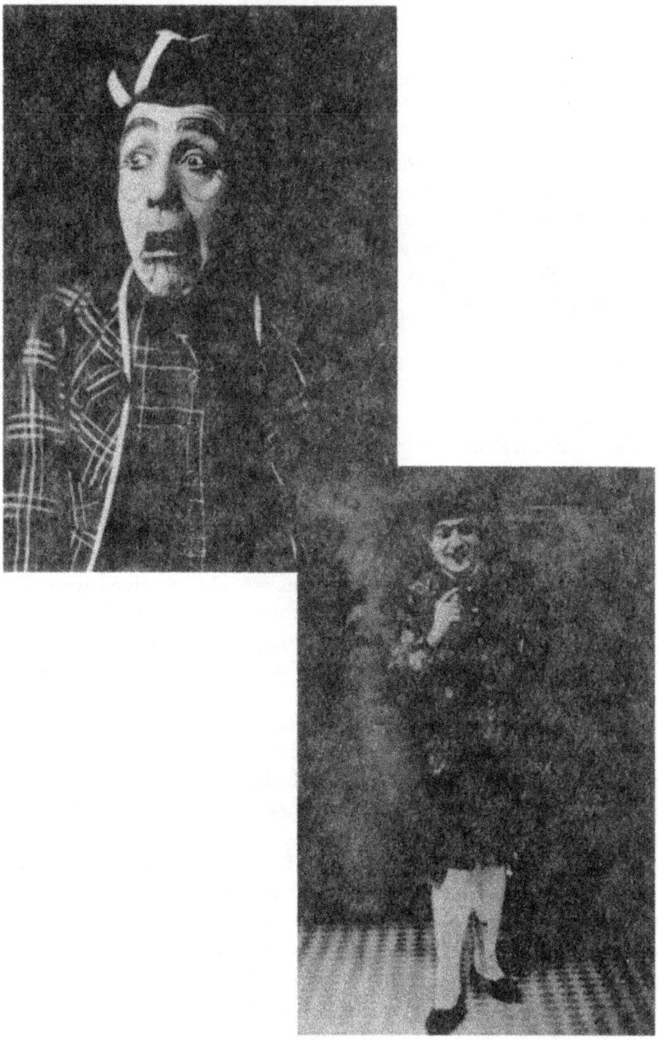

Alfred Aratoli and Arturo Godi

18. THE STENTERELLATE

The titles of the Stenterellate are not merely suggestive—they are expository; they summarized the entire plot. The opening play introduced another stock character of the popular Italian theatre, Pasquariello, who acted as foil to Stenterello in *L'Incontro di Pasquariello e Stenterello, tormentati dall'articolo 139* (*The Meeting of Pasquariello and Stenterello, Tormented by Article 139*). Pasquariello, of Sicilian origin, is a minor, attenuated *carattere*. In the Commedia dell'Arte he was a stupid valet, a double for Scaramuccia. His role was played in San Francisco by Cesare.

We have mentioned the excessive length of Italian programs. Besides the Stenterellate the program generally included musical numbers (violin solos, operatic duets, romanze and arias), moving pictures, a melodrama, or a comedy. Thus in May, one of the performances exhibited the marital difficulties of our two heroes, Stenterello and Pasquariello, in the role of *Mariti sfortunati* (*Unfortunate Husbands*) after serveral operatic arias, violin solos, "emotional drama," and other treats. During July one of these melodramas, *Il Lampionario de porto* (*The Lamp-Lighter of the Harbor*) was presented in addition to the comedy *Stenterello servitore de quattro padroni* (*Stenterello, Servant of Four Masters*) in which the agitated factotum anxiously tried to satisfy the boisterous whims of his French, English, Spanish, and Italian masters.

In many of these plays Stenterello suggests the celebrated Beaumarchais valet, Figaro, the Barber of Seville, who is always intervening in complicated intrigues and setting things to right. The prodigiousness of Stenterello's deeds, moreover, are amazingly incongruous with his humble station. *Stenterello fruttivendolo e salvatore della patria* (*Stenterello, Fruit-Seller and Savior of the Country*) is one of the favorite Stenterellate. His ups and downs are vertiginous; sometimes he is a lowly garbage man, at other times a *gran signore e ganimede per burla* (great lord and dandy in jest).

At times during the season Pasquariello was permitted to star. The evening after Stenterello exhausted himself playing servant to four masters, Cesare assumed a fantastic sounding role; he was *Pasquariello madre senze figli e zia senza nipoti* (*Pasquariello, Mother Without Children and Aunt Without Nephews*). In August one of the authentic characters of the Commedia dell'Arte was presented to San Francisco; this was Pulcinello, the popular Neapolitan clown who appeared in the somber-sounding comedy, *La Fucilzione di Pulcinella* (*The Shooting of Pulcinella*).

19. LARGE AND VARIED REPERTOIRES

In addition to the Stenterellate, opera was stressed, usually in the popular sugar-coated form of isolated arias and duets. On June 13th two new members of the company had their debut; these were the young operatic singers, Adolfo Mariotti, tenor, and Adelina Dosseno, soprano. They sang a group of arias following a two-act comedy by Scarpetta, *La Balia* (*The Nurse*). Mariotti and Dosseno in turn were followed by moving pictures and variety numbers.

Well-known dramas were also given by the Cesare Company; on June 16th the popular leading lady of the company, Signora Palange, played at her benefit the suffering Camille of *La Signora delle Camelie*. On this special occasion prices were raised slightly: for adults it was now 10 cents and 20 cents; for children still 5 cents. After a while prices remained at this moderate level.

In August the popular classic of the American stage, *The Two Orphans*, was given in its almost equally popular Italian version, *Le Due Orfanelle*. Occasionally original plays were presented: On September 7th, in addition to the drama *Il Cappriccio di un Padre* (*A Father's Caprice*) and a farce, *La Tigre di Bengala* (*The Bengal Tiger*), a drama in two acts, *Caino e Abele* (written by a member of the cast, Mario Scarpa) was presented.

Out of the tremendous repertoire of Stenterellate that had been accumulating since 1775 most of the actors who played Stenterello had had their *fatica "particolare"*—their specialties. On September 9, 1909 the Cesare Company had a *sera di gala* and presented Godi in the impressive-sounding melodrama, *Stenterello servo del diavolo ovvero la ciece ed il gioielliere* (*Stenterello, Servant of the Devil, or, The Blind Woman and the Jeweler*).

The Compagnia Comica-Drammatica of Cesare continued to play at the Washngton Square until the middle of 1910, dazzling their public every night with the brilliance and fecundity of their talents. At length the novelty wore off; the capricious public began to demand new faces, and Stenterello and his troupe left for other parts of the country. They had had great popular success. They had established the Italian theatre of San Francisco on a permanent footing, but they did not take a fortune away with them. These were no longer the days of the gold rush; these were the days when people paid 5 cents and 10 cents and expected to see a four-hour show of variety, farce, tragedy, comedy, and Stenterello.

20. SHAKESPEARE IN NORTH BEACH

The Maori Company followed Cesare's Company into the Washington Square Theatre in August 1910. Antonio Maori had had great success in New York. A great actor, for years he maintained the highest traditions of the *teatro di prose* in America. It was, of course, Signora Alessandro who first secured his engagement. His company in San Francisco had no singers, no dancers, no comedians, not even Stenterello. Maori simply produced legitimate dramas; he made no compromise with public taste—and he created a new high level for the Italian theatre.

The period between 1910 to 1912 in which the Compagnia Maori played nightly, with a complete change of program every night, was the highest point ever reached by the Italian theatre in San Francisco. Maori established the legitimate theatre in North Beach; what is more, he brought Shakespeare to North Beach and the citizens revelled in it. This was a higher-class theatre than the Stenterellate, and prices were raised accordingly out of the nickelodeon class to the more "dignified" level of 15 cents to 75 cents. The Washington Square Theatre advertised itself as the only legitimate theatre in San Francisco changing its program every evening, with two changes on Saturday and Sunday.

During their season at the Washington Square, the capable and untiring Maori Company swung breathlessly through the stock repertoire of European drama. They performed Dumas, Goethe, Schontau, Sudermann, Sardou, Shakespeare, and others, besides native Italian dramas. Many of the plays were much too pretentious for the small company. Some of them demanded a large cast of characters, and because the company was limited, it was customary for many of the actors to play two, three, or sometimes even four parts in a single play. For an Italian this is not as difficult as it sounds. All it required was that the prompter have a good voice and the actors energy, skill, and imagination.

Plays by Dumas or those adapted from his novels were favorites of the European stage and were among the most popular of the Maori repertoire. One of these, given in September 1910, was the romantic drama based on the life of the English actor, Kean: *Kean ovvero genio e sregolatezza* (*Kean, or, Genius and Disorder*). This play has seventeen characters and five acts. During the fourth act there is a theatre scene where Kean, as Hamlet, declaims the well-known soliloquy. Maori's casting of this play is very significant. It reveals the Italian principal of doubling in roles; it also reveals the secret of the homogeneity of the Italian company.

21. THE MAORI COMPANY

In *Kean*, Antonio Maori (the *capo comico* or head of the company) played the protagonist; his wife, Concetta, played opposite him, along with his daughter, Maria. There were three members of the Pinto family in the play, one of whom played two parts, and two Francos, one playing two roles. Mario Scarpa played two roles. In the play also, were Silvio Minciotti and Ester Cunico, who later were married, had two daughters, and thus erected the framework of the Compagnia Minciotti.

This intermarriage of players, traditional in the Italian theatre, explains the remarkable homogeneity of Italian troupes. Children and grandchildren generally followed in the footsteps of their forebears. The same role was often handed down through generations. Successive intermarriages strengthened the cohesion of the troupe, which was often a patriarchal group headed by the father—the leading actor, the *capo comico*, the director, and teacher. His wife usually played opposite him. In the company were the children, the in-laws, and the grandchildren—who were being groomed to succeed their ancestors. Usually the actors played the same roles on and off stage. Columbine was Harlequin's wife in real life as well as on the stage. Most Italian plays, in fact, dealt with husband-wife situations. These circumstances enhanced the naturalness of the acting.

22. THE POPULARITY OF SHAKESPEARE

Shakespeare found an important place in the repertoire of the Maori Company. There was at least one "Italianized" version of Shakespeare performed each week. In the course of their season at the Washington Square, practically all of Shakespeare's works were given. The favorites with the Italian public, quite naturally, were those with Italian themes or Italian settings. What the drama-loving Italians appreciated and admired most in Shakespeare was the obvious dramatic quality, the passion—and the violence.

At the time of this writing there was still a tradition of Shakespeare in Italy. An annual Shakespearean festival was held in the Public Square of Venice, where were performed *Othello*, *The Merchant of Venice*, and *King Lear*. Shakespeare became popular in Italy through the art of her great actors. It was Ruggiero, for example, who popularized the Italian interpretations of Hamlet and Macbeth. Many important actors such as Gustavo Salvini, son of the great Tommaso, limited themselves exclusively to a Shakespearean repertoire.

Certain plays have been more popular than others. *Othello* was, perhaps, more of a favorite in Italy than anywhere else. The theme of this tragedy (translated into grand opera—definite proof of its having reached the center of Italian hearts) is passion and jealousy. It is a husband-wife drama, almost purely an Italian tragedy, and it is, perhaps, more easily comprehensible to the Italian than to the English mind. *The Merchant of Venice*, with its setting and theme of revenge, is another Italian favorite. *Romeo and Juliet*, although located in Italy, was not overwhelmingly popular. The subject of *Romeo and Juliet*, young, romantic love, scarcely found its way onto the Italian stage, which involved itself more often with the emotional complications of grown-up married people. The Italian theatre was not concerned with elegiac sentiments and lyrical swoonings, but with the crude throbbings of mature passion. *The Taming of the Shrew*, on the other hand, was extremely popular; its unsentimental ridicule of marriage is an ancient Latin theme.

All these plays were given by the Maori Company with great success. At times, however, the critics were antagonistic. During November 1910, Maori played *Hamlet* for three consecutive nights, an unusually lengthy run in the Italian theatre, and incontrovertible proof of the play's popularity. The critic of *L'Italia*, however, pronounced Maori's characterizations of Othello and Shylock to be much better. He considered *Amleto* somewhat "too intellectual for the North Beach audience, a play better read than recited." According to the critic, Maori did not interpret the role properly, and did not give Hamlet sufficient "profundity, melancholy and mystery." Concetta Maori, however, was found to be capably tragic as Ophelia. Scarpa was sympathetic in the role of Horatio, while la Cunica was sacrificed in the role of the Queen. On the whole, concluded the critic, Shakespeare is suited neither to public taste nor to public intelligence. He urged the production of minor works. But Maori continued to produce Shakespeare and the audiences ignored the metaphysical and recondite passages and applauded the melodramatic action and the vigorous death scenes. The Italians were pleased by Shakespeare; they liked their theatre "theatrical."

23. THE MAORI REPERTOIRE

Otello and *Kean* were two characteristic offerings of a typical Maori week. On Sunday, September 11, 1910 *Il Ratto delle Savine* (*The Rape of the Sabine*) was performed in the matinee; in the evening another comedy, *L'Avvocato e il pizzicagnolo* (*The Lawyer and the Pork-Butcher*). On Monday, *Kean*; Tuesday, a French farce, *Il Deputato de Bombignac* (*The Deputy of Bombignac*); Wednesday, a request performance of *Otello*; Thursday, the Italian version of *The Two Orphans*. This drama was advertised as a spectacle play with 23 characters, soldiers, common people and citizens. The prices were reduced for this special occasion. The new "popular prices" were: gallery, 10 cents; pit, 20 cents; individual seats, 30 cents; and boxes, 50 cents.

On Friday another favorite Dumas play was given, *Una Notte a Firenze* (*A Night in Florence*), and prices went back to the old level—15 cents to 75 cents. On Saturday, two performances: comedy in the afternoon—Guarini's *Madama 4 Soldi* (*Mme 4-Penny*), in the evening—the drama *La Signora delle Camelie* (*Camille*). The week ended with the performance of another French favorite, Sardou's *Fédora* at Sunday matinee, and an Italian comedy, Scarpetta's *Il Romanzo d'un Farmacista Povero* (*The Romance of a Poor Pharmacist*) at night.

This very full and varied week is typical; very rarely was a performance repeated before the exacting audience. However, if a piece proved very successful it might be repeated once or twice during the week, as we have seen in the case of *Amleto*. During October *Romanticismo*, a drama by the Italian Rovetta, was played on a Tuesday and Wednesday at "popular prices." During this month also the Maori Company temporarily deserted alien sources and played other popular plays by Italian writers: Busnelli's *La Monaca di Cracovia* (*The Nun of Cracow*); Gualtieri's five-act melodrama *I Misteri dell'Inquisizione di Spagna* (*The Mysteries of the Spanish Inquisition*); as well as several original one-act plays and farces by members of the Italian colony in San Francisco.

Grande serate and *serate straordinarie* were given with regularity and frequency, on the occasion of benefits and special performances. On one of these dates (October 20, 1910), Concetta Maori, the leading lady of the company, was honored; she played the title role of Sudermann's famous drama, *Magda* (known in the Italian repertoire as *Casa Paterna*). On another occasion several months later *Giulietta e Romeo* was given for the first time with the Maoris, husband and wife, playing the star-crossed lovers.

Sometimes the customers of the Washington Square were presented with unexpected and bizarre treats. One evening during January 1911, *Faust* was performed by the Maori Company. The next evening was a *serata straordinaria*; the performance for the evening included Beaumarchais' *Barber of Seville*, which was followed by a wrestling match between the Italian champion, Piombo, and the German, Gōtsch. In describing this performance, the dramatic critic of the Italian newspaper devoted six paragraphs to the wrestling match and one paragraph to the play. Probably the wrestling match was a more finished performance.

24. THE ITALIAN THEATRE INACTIVE

The Maori Company played through 1912. Then the Italian theatre, which had been steaming ahead so triumphantly, came to an abrupt pause, an interruption characteristic of its uneven career in San Francisco. Maori returned to New York, his company disbanded; some of the members such as Minciotti and la Cunico formed their own companies and went on tour. Others, like Scarpa, joined the troupe of Mimi Aguglia then playing in San Francisco. In March l'Aguglia came to San Francisco and bestowed a new brilliance on the Italian theatre; she played a short two-week season at the Cort Theatre for the Americans and then returned to her countrymen and played three months in North Beach. Mimi Aguglia was an internationally famous tragedienne and her appeal was not restricted to Italians; her visits to San Francisco are much more significant to the development of the more specialized Teatro Italiano—the subsidized theatre, the theatre for the elite—than to the popular theatre of North Beach—the theatre whose only sponsor is the capricious will of the public. For this reason the career of Mimi Aguglia in San Francisco will be treated more fully in the section on the Teatro Italiano.

Then l'Aguglia was gone, and for a time the Italian theatre came almost to a complete standstill. Between 1914 and 1917 it was quiescent in North Beach. Occasional performances were organized by Oreste Seragnoli Scarpa and other remnants of the Maori and Aguglia troupes at the Washington Square Theatre and the social halls; but without sufficiently strong management and organization, very little could be accomplished.

25. THE LIBERTY THEATRE

In the meantime the Washington Square Theatre had slipped from the hands of the Italians and was being run as an American moving picture and vaudeville house. Things looked black for the Italian theatre. But in reality there was no cause for great anxiety—for Signora Antonietta Pisanelli Alessandro was still in San Francisco.

The Signora Impresario had not been idle these past few years. In her typical energetic fashion she had been scrambling about town, erecting and renting theatres; negotiating here, there, and everywhere; installing a Chinese theatre in Chinatown with one hand; with the other arranging for the reception of a Spanish theatre from Mexico. Her deepest interests, however, were with the Italian theatre; and now she came to its rescue. By an extraordinary manipulation of finances, a *coup de maître*, she got control of the California Theatre on Broadway, between Grant Avenue and Stockton Street. Renamed the Liberty Theatre, it became the new home of the Italian theatre in San Francisco. Here, in January 1917, the Compagnia Italiana de Matienzo played a three-month engagement.

26. TERESA DE MATIENZO AND ALFRED ARATOLI

Signora Alessandro had started her career in the theatre as a *cantatrice*; Teresa de Matienzo, too, was a famous singer of Neapolitan songs. She had with her a strong, proficient company that could supplement her folk songs and ballads with robust performances of all the popular dramas. One of the most popular was the four-act *emozionante dramma* of Victorien Sardou, *La Tosca*. Although repeated many times, *Tosca* always secured a favorable response from the audience. The program of January 23 reveals one or two old names; also some newcomers who were to add luster to the Italian theatre of San Francisco. The following is the cast:

>Scarpia—C. Tricoli
>Cavaradossi—M. Scarpa
>Azelotti—O. Seragnoli
>Eusebio—A. Aratoli
>Gennarino—S. Mezzacapo
>Colometti—L. Poggi
>Schiarrone—A. Cacciarelli
>Tosca—R. Bernardini

The *Voce del Populo* (which had been displeased by the company's pedestrian performance of Scarpetta's three-act Neapolitan comedy, *Scarpetta*) was gratified by its splendid recovery in *Tosca*. The critic found Rosina Bernardini, the protagonist, to have been somewhat cold in manner at the start of her performance, only to become more animated as the play progressed. He was especially impressed by her vocal delivery: "Her correct method of enunciation, without jumbling the words together—a very common defect of our theatre—left nothing to desire, and she deserves much praise." Scarpa did a good job, although he was handicapped by miscasting. Tricoli was competent as Scarpia. Aratoli was good, although his voice was faulty on this occasion. Seragnoli was thorough in his character part.

As usual, the drama was preceded by several irrelevant musical numbers. De Matienzo sang her popular Neapolitan airs; she was assisted in her duets by Signora Rondera and Signor Alfred Aratoli. And thus was Aratoli introduced to San Francisco. Aratoli, who a few months after the departure of Signora de Matienzo, was to have his own City of Florence Company playing at the Liberty, bringing Stenterello again to North Beach.

27. THE RETURN OF STENTERELLO

Aratoli brought new color, movement, and brilliance to North Beach. His Città di Firenze Company was a versatile and active body of troupers capable of producing almost any kind of entertainment at a moment's notice; anything from Stenterello farces to blood-curdling tragedy, from light opera to Passion Plays, from grand opera to Shakespeare. The company included the *capo comico*, Alfredo Aratoli, a master of pantomime, a devastating Stenterello, a brilliant exponent of the Florentine dialect comedies; Ida Aratoli, his wife, a clever leading lady in operetta, comedy, and farce; Antonio Grillo, who had played in Florence, Rome, Naples, and New York; Camilla Brunetta, *cantatrice* of Neapolitan songs; Vittorina, who had performed at the Folies Bergères and in Florence and New York. There was Roose, who specialized in operatic arias, and Baldo Minuti, "*bravo cantatore ed elegante attore.*" All of them were experienced and accomplished, resourceful, amazingly versatile, capable one day of romping about in lowly comedy, climbing the next day into exalted tragedy. All of them could sing as well as act. Their singing and their acting were uneven and unrefined, but full of fire, zest and exuberance. In April and May they played a hectic season at the Liberty which included almost every kind of theatrical genre imaginable. One evening the actors strutted about with flourishes in *Otello*; the next day they cavorted in a *grande stenerellata*, in which Aratoli impersonated *Stenterello, La Cavolaia di Firenze* (*The Garbage-man of Florence*). Before Easter they impulsively staged a Passion Play—nothing was too grandiose, nothing too lowly for them to attempt. *La Morte e Passione di N. S. Gesu' Cristo* was a spectacular production. It had eight acts and innumerable characters; and at least half of North Beach made up the mob scenes.

28. THE PASSION PLAY

A Passion Play given by Italians is essentially different from one produced by the Germans. With the Latins it is a gay, rhetorical feast, not solemn, but a spectacle, riotous with florid colors and flamboyant gestures. The Italian approach to spiritual matters is a theatrical one, as anybody knows who has ever witnessed an Italian wedding or funeral; Latins are fond of festival and pageantry. The Passion Play is typical of a theatrical enthusiasm which usually exceeds technical resources.

The company had a few rehearsals, the prompter was furnished with the script, the carpenters hastily threw up the necessary sets, and everybody flung themselves into the proper exalted mood. The young actor, Carlo Tricoli, played Christus; Aratoli, the comedian, played the role of Pontius Pilate; Scarpa, who in recent years had been gaining weight and developing into a proficient "heavy," was quite at home in the part of Judas; Maria Magdalena was played by Ester Minciotti; and Veronica by Ida Aratoli.

The drama was making excellent progress, accompanied by excited shouting and gesticulating, and with only a few minor accidents, until it arrived at the momentous scene on Calvary. Then Tricoli as the crucified Christ suddenly felt a sinking sensation. He glanced down and learned that he *was* sinking, that the block which supported him on the cross had been insecurely fastened and was slipping down. Tricoli took a deep breath and began to curse heartily in a very voluble Italian, *sotto voce*, summoning his prototype to witness his predicament. Beneath the cross knelt Maria Magdalena and Veronica, their pious lamentations interrupted by the frenzied profanity of the martyred Christ. The rest of the cast were in the wings, bursting with suppressed laughter. They found no blasphemy in the spectacle of Christ apparently cursing his mother. They did not take their religion too solemnly, but accepted it as a part of a large, earthy existence.

When the curtain fell on the Passion Play, an exhausted and indignant Tricoli was hauled down from the cross, swearing a solemn and vigorous oath that hereafter he would devote himself to less taxing occupations than impersonating the Lord. But in 1919 at the Washington Square Theatre, and again in 1926 at the Silesian Auditorium, he was dragged away from other pursuits to enact the role of Christ in increasingly more spectacular and more hazardous plays of the Passion. He was too good an actor to retire so easily.

29. CARLO TRICOLI

Carlo Tricoli was an impressive Christus—he was so effective that Father Paperni would grant Aratoli's company the use of the basement of the Church of St. Peter and Paul for their performance of the Passion Play on Easter, 1926, only on condition that to Tricoli alone the role of the Lord would be entrusted. By this time Tricoli had abandoned the theatre for the less artistic and more secure profession of law.

The law was Tricoli's original vocation, the theatre a temporary digression. He had come from Sicily to New York as a boy in 1901. An interest in the stage had been satisfied initially by amateur theatricals, and he was studying for the law, when, in 1912, he married the daughter of Gustavo Raggazino, an impresario. The marriage changed his life. His new environment, together with the necessity of earning a living for a rapidly growing family, led him to desert his studies. He went on the professional stage, playing in New York, Philadelphia, Boston, and Chicago. By 1914 he had appeared in an early silent film with the famous actress, Mary Pickford. He was an extremely handsome leading man and consequently was in great demand.

In 1917 Tricoli came to San Francisco with the De Matienzo troupe. When it left he stayed on as a member of the Aratoli Company. For two years he played at the Liberty and the Washington Square, with the traditional expansiveness and versatility of his race, in light opera, drama, and grand opera. He made a credible Hamlet when he played with the Compagnia Drammatica Aratoli at the Libery in June 1917. In March 1918, after a short trip East, he rejoined Aratoli to make his debut in Giacometti's *La Morte Civile*. On August 23, 1918 he played Osvaldo in *Gli Spettri*, Ibsen's *Ghosts*, which had been made popular in Italy by the performance of the famous actor Ermete Zacconi; in his characterization of the tortured Oswald the young Tricoli displayed unusual insight and penetration. Opposite him were other distinguished actors: Amelia Brunetti, Tina Modotti, Oreste Seragnoli, and Gigi Mattioli. A week later, at a special performance given as a benefit for Italian war victims, he played with the same cast in another popular Italian play, *La Nemica*, as Roberto, the son who is tormented by his mother's guilt and must condemn her as his enemy. Then, on March 7, 1919, at a benefit for Silvio Minciotti at the Washington Square he played another somber role—that of the tragic Neri in *La Cena delle Beffe*. In this role, declared *L'Italia*, Tricoli was a revelation, "so efficacious and inspired was his interpretation of this difficult role."

30. BLACKSTONE VS. THE "BOARDS"

In August 1919, Tricoli, seeking a new medium, made his English-speaking debut at the Alcazar Theatre. At the same time he deserted his usual tragic roles—playing the part of a rich and ardent South American in the musical comedy *Here Comes the Bride*.

But roles, whether in English or in Italian, were becoming scarce and unremunerative, and the Tricoli family was steadily increasing. So in 1920, when he was offered an opportunity to work in the legal department of the Italian Consulate and to complete his legal studies, he willingly abandoned the stage. Two years later he was admitted to the bar. However Carlo Tricoli was so talented an actor that the North Beach public was reluctant to let him go; and he himself was not altogether released from the grip of the theatre. He continued to give occasional performances at such times as the call became too strong to resist. Despite an increasing law practice he appeared during the years to come in various benefits. In 1925 he directed a performance of *Otello* given by an amateur group of the Unione Sportiva Italiana Virtus Club; he himself was the protagonist of the tragedy.

Carlo Tricoli (at the writing of this monograph) held the office of Assistant District Attorney of San Francisco, while maintaining an extensive private practice. But he still found time to make brief returns to the theatre of North Beach. On October 22, 1931 he played opposite Argentina Ferraù in *La Casa del Peccato* (*The House of Crime*) a drama by a local playwright, Paolo Pallavicini, given for the first time at the Teatro Milano. In the cast were Seragnoli, playing the lover, and little Lidia Tricolo, playing Giselda. Lidia, although only six, was already a veteran of the stage, having made her debut a year before at the Liberty Theatre as "Sonny Boy" in an Italian musical drama adapted from Al Jolson's film.

31. STENTERELLO BECOMES PASSÉ

In 1919, after his first short season at the Liberty Theatre, Aratoli returned to New York. The season was notable in that Aratoli, who had identified himself almost exclusively with the figure of Stenterello, had been forced to assume other roles—in operetta, drama, comedy, grand opera. Stenterello was losing his popularity.

The world had changed very rapidly in the decades preceding, and Stenterello, who for the past 150 years had been an indispensable prop of the Florentine theatre, now seemed outdated. The tradition had died and Stenterello was no longer a living link of the past with the present, but a slightly ridiculous museum relic. Stenterello was very Italian and very human, but at the same time he was of the eighteenth century and he spoke the dialect of the eighteenth century. In the Italian colonies of America, as the bonds with Italian traditions became gradually weaker, Stenterello could not compete with the more smoothly sophisticated cinema. The educated Italian-American tended to feel a superior contempt for the figures of the Commedia dell'Arte and the puppet show because of their naïveté.

32. FARFARIELLO COMES WEST

The Italian fascination with stock characters, however, created an appropriate substitute for Stenterello. Soon after Aratoli left North Beach it was announced that, after a successful tour of the country, the famous Farfariello was coming to San Francisco. La Signora Impresario had scored another *coup*.

Edoardo Migliaccio was an old friend of the Signora's. She had made his acquaintance back in 1895 when the young immigrant boy from Salerno first arrived in New York. Migliaccio knew firsthand the comic, pathetic struggles of the immigrant who, without knowledge of English and without pronounced brilliance, must somehow make a living, experiences which became valuable material for his later Farfariello *macchiete*. His first job was as a lining-presser in a Jewish sweat shop on the East Side. The job lasted less than one day because Migliaccio, in a moment of distraction (or, more likely, while writing a poem), permitted the iron to burn a large hole in the lining. Out on the street once again, and considering briefly the prospects of his future success in industry, Migliaccio made the prompt (and wise) decision to go into the theatre.

He had already written several skits and songs. One was about a character "Farfariello," a ludicrous burlesque of various immigrant types. Eventually the young Migliaccio was discovered by Signora Antonietta Pisanelli as she was auditioning a duet partner in a little theatre on Mulberry Street. It was here, at 108 Mulberry Street, that Farfariello made his debut, beginning a career that took him triumphantly back and forth across the continent and eventually made him the rage of music halls and *teatri di varietà* in Italy.

33. THE FARFARIELLO MACCHIETE

Stenterello was Italy of the eighteenth century; Farfariello was "Little Italy" of the twentieth century—the immigrant of New York's East Side, and of San Francisco's North Beach. Farfariello was a product of American life, yet he belonged to the tradition of the Italian theatre. Edoardo Migliaccio created a character with a life independent of the personality of the creator. Farfariello was of the tradition of Harlequin, of Scaramouche, of Stenterello, of Charlie Chaplin.

Stenterello was the Florentine man-in-the-street, who in various roles commented ironically and satirically on his social status and on the life around him. Farfariello appeared in *macchiete* sketches which included action, pantomime and singing, and that poked fun at characteristic types in the Italian colony—the iceman, the garbage collector, the watchman, the nurse, etc. Farfariello was "modern," but he was also the product of a long evolution. One of the programs of the time quotes a New York critic:

> If Farfariello is "up to the minute" in his sketches from New York life there is something about the technique of his art that suggests a century of tradition as its basis. It is medieval in its realistic satire and its essentially robust comedy. Rather than to characterize it as realistic, however, one should say that it is caricature based on a close observation of the actual.

The Italian newspapers greeted the creation of their countryman with enthusiastic bravos. Luigi Lucatelli, New York correspondent of *Il Secolo di Milano* wrote to Italy:

> ...Migliaccio, surnamed Farfariello, has created with words, music, costume and makeup the most delightful colonial sketches that can be imagined. Every aspect—ironic, serious or gay, joyous or grotesque, of colonial life—has traversed the art of this young man of genius. From the little shopkeeper *parvenu*, decked out in the uniform of a general, to the *cafone* who comments on current topics and argues with the American who discredits the far-off fatherland, the simple and stubborn spirit, gayly bizarre, or a little veiled in melancholy, comes to us through his art, not as in a series of vast can-

> vases, but as a collection of water colors of subtle color and tone....

And *Il Giornale Italiano* of New York commented on the education to be gleaned from the study of Farfariello:

> If I wished to acquaint a foreigner with the psychology, somewhat grotesque yet full of common sense, tenacious to the ideal of race, good-natured, gay and rugged, of the *cafone* acclimated in America....I would have to speak two hours and to have the eloquence of a Demosthenes, or massacre the reader with two columns of prose. But if I led him to see "The *Cafone* Reasons" recited by Edoardo Migliaccio, or Farfariello, all this little world somewhat distorted, somewhat sullied by local speech and customs, but full of an indestructible *Italiana*, would reveal itself with a marvelous limpid, lively truth....He has written the true story of the Italian colony in America, and he has carved in his *Bosso* in this image of this mass in continual transformation, with a very subtle and facile art.

34. FARFARIELLO: AMBASSADOR FROM LITTLE ITALY

Stenterello was an adjunct of the more formal *Teatro di Prosa* (legitimate theatre) in Florence; Farfariello represents the lively, impromptu *Teatro di Varietà* (variety theatre) in New York. Migliaccio, with his facility for creating his own lyrics and his own music, belongs to the minstrel tradition. But he is essentially a product of the Italian people and of their robust, spontaneous Commedia dell'Arte.

Stenterello died, and even Farfariello, a creation of the Italian-American, could not survive in his abruptly changing *milieu*. The *colono* rapidly became Americanized. As the immigrant discarded his native language and customs, his psychology likewise changed.

But in 1917 and 1918 Italian immigrants were pouring by the hordes into the country—and crowds were filling the Liberty Theatre in San Francisco to laugh at the brilliant mimicry of Migliaccio. Farfariello was a familiar phenomenon, who with ludicrous make-up and costume, with grimaces, gestures, and guitar, ridiculed their language, their mannerisms, and their customs. He was a familiar character, typical of the *cafone*, who adopted American clothes, aped American manners and even took over a few American colloquialisms, but who was still Italian to the core. Some of Farfariello's humor had to do with uses and abuses of language, ridiculing the immigrants' tendency to Italianize English words and to incorporate them into his language: Thus "elevator" became "leveta," "car" became "carro," "Van Ness" became "Vannesi," and so on. This was the immigrant's way of entering a strange new world by a familiar and well-used road.

More of Farfariello's humor lay in his shrewd, often ironical comments on the changed social position of the *cafone* in America. He was impressed by the differences between American democracy and the fixed caste system of Europe. One of Farfariello's favorite songs was "La Sciabola":

> *Questo mondo è così combinato*
> *Il cafone qui conta di più*
> *Il blasone non viene apprezzato,*
> *Danno ai calli maggiore virtù.*
> *Li la sciabola l'usa il signore*
> *Per vertenze d'onore appiana*
> *Ma c'ca è se'ietta sudore*
> *Qui la sciabola serve a zappa.*

Rendered into English, the point, depending upon a pun, is hopelessly lost. *Sciabola* in Italy means "sabre," and in the dialect of the Italian-American laborer, "shovel." Freely translated:

> *This new world is upside-down*
> *And the cafone here can smile*
> *For the coat-of-arms has no renown*
> *and callouses are in style.*
> *There the signore raises the sabre*
> *When his sacred honor's hurt*
> *But here the shovel's used in labor*
> *And raises mainly dirt.*

But most of Farfariello's importance was in his caricatures of Italian-American types. All the various types in the Italian colony were game for him: the fruit dealer, the grocer, the watchman, etc. He occasionally gave parodies on famous personalities, such as Enrico Caruso. He was a superb impersonator of female types: the schoolgirl, *la nutrice* (the nurse), Donna Vicenza, Donna Rosa, the Sicilian. His studies were often burlesques, often coarse, but they were true-to-life, and those he was laughing at laughed the loudest.

Farfariello came to San Francisco with his own company, but he alone was practically an entire *Teatro di Varietà*. His work had a rigorous artistic basis and, as an interpretation of one phase of American life—that transitory period between immigration and Americanization—it deserves to be known to the wider American public.

35. THE CAREER OF TINA MODOTTI

In 1918 Farfariello left San Francisco to continue his American triumphs, and then to be hailed throughout Italy as a great colonial artist. Italy had sent Stenterello to America; Edoardo Migliaccio returned the favor with Farfariello.

Stars came and went, but the old guard remained firm in North Beach. Seragnoli, Scarpa, and other permanent settlers continued to give performances at the Liberty and at the Washington Square, together with a newcomer, Amelia Bruno. In July 1918 the actors joined forces to create the new Compagnia Bruno-Seragnoli. They gave a short season of popular drama at the Washington Square Theatre, including such favorite melodramas as *Tosca*, *La Rivoluzione Russ*, *and Dall'Ombre al Sole*. It was a routine season, eventful only in that the fabulous Tina Modotti made her last appearance before an enchanted Italian public. She gave one of her best performances as the pathetic heroine of Niccodemi's drama *Scampolo*.

Those who remember Tina Modotti as a young immigrant girl in San Francisco recall principally that she was beautiful though eccentric, possessing a number of striking talents. A promising career as a *modiste* was terminated by the call of the more glamorous stage. In the Compagnia Città de Firenze she played with Aratoli, Tricoli, Seragnoli and Gigi Mattioli. Immediately her beauty, her distinction, and her ability attracted attention. *L'Italia* of March 2, 1918 commended her excellent diction and acting ability in her role as the young daughter of the convict in *La Morte Civile*. In *Spettri* the "*brava e grazioza* Tina Modotti was altogether delightful in the small role of Regina."

Modotti very rapidly improved in her grasp of the theatre, and as a "personality" she became very popular in the Italian colony. In its review of *La Nemica*, *L'Italia* (August 29, 1918) called special attention to the young actress, who was playing the modest role of Marta Regnault:

> Tina Modotti, whom all in our colony have so often admired and whom we may say, we all love as much for her goodness as for her brilliant artistic qualities....She is still at the beginning of her career...and yesterday surprised even her warmest admirers by the dramatic intensity of her acting, especially in the great final scene of the second act....Always careful, conscientious....Signora Modotti has already obtained—if we may so phrase it—her diploma as an artist and continuing to study as she does her career is assured.

And probably Tina might have gone far in the theatre had not one of the most ardent of her admirers, a young French-Canadian poet, intervened. He and Tina were married and left San Francisco for Los Angeles. Soon Tina had found a new medium for her self-expression. She began writing poems that were good enough to be published in the *Dial*—while her young man got employment in the checkroom of a Hollywood cabaret. Shortly after he died of tuberculosis.

36. NEW MUSES AND A CALLING

Tina Modotti, of the dark, tragic eyes, found Mexico. There she studied painting and sculpture, and posed for some of Diego Rivera's most famous murals. Then photography lured her. She posed for the famous photographer, Edward Weston, and began serious work herself in this new field.

Tina Modotti was more than a chameleon; she took on not only the color of her atmosphere, but she also absorbed her *milieu* entirely. In Mexico City, as she was beginning to acquire a considerable reputation as a photographer, she became acquainted with a famous labor leader—and she was reborn a revolutionary. She lived a dangerous, frantic life, delivering eloquent, impassioned speeches in Spanish to Mexican crowds. She was repeatedly imprisoned by the authorities, but that did not deter her. Finally, her lover was murdered by an assassin's bullet at her feet on a Mexico City street. There was a sensational trial, and Tina fled the country.

Now Russia became her refuge, and she discovered a new interest—the cinema. Her work in the Russian cinema, most importantly, her film on the Baku region, was widely acclaimed.

It is difficult now to record the vicissitudes of this extraordinary woman. The friends of her youth in San Francisco eventually lost contact with her. Rumors had her flying wildly about, always in the thick of every European intrigue. At the time of this writing, she was reported to be in war-torn Spain doing propaganda work for the Loyalists, no longer young and beautiful, but still burning for art and life—and revolution.

Her life as an adventuress had the superficial glamor of that of a Lola Montez[3] or an Adah Menken,[4] but her talents were sincere and genuine. She was beautiful and gifted, and something of a genius. She lived many lives and had many careers. She seems to have excelled in everything she attempted. As an actress her penetrating interpretation of *Scampolo* was long remembered by devotees of the theatre in North Beach with awe.

Yet back in 1918 no one could have foretold that little Tina Modotti, the ingénue of the Compagnia Bruno-Seragnoli, was about to mature through the diverse metamorphoses of poet-artist-photographer to revolutionary.

And soon, like so many other troupes, the Bruno-Seragnoli Company disintegrated and was no more in San Francisco. Drama, too, suffered a temporary decline; for now came the era of "two-bit" opera in Washington Square.

37. "TWO BIT" OPERA

In 1919 Amelia Bruno organized the La Moderna Comic Opera Company. In the troupe were some of the old actors: Ida Aratoli, Ester Minciotti, Frank Puglia, Oreste Seragnoli, and Carlo Tricoli. They put on such well-known operettas as *La Duchesse du Bal Tabarin* and *La Vedova Allegra* (*The Merry Widow*). Soon there was a Moderne Grand Opera Company; then there was The Latin Quarter Opera Company offering opera four nights a week. *La Traviata, Aida, Rigoletto, La Favorite, L'Elisir d'Amore*—all the operas in the Italian repertoire were given for 25 cents admission!

Never, in the distinguished career of opera in San Francisco, has there been such popular enthusiasm for this massive art form—and certainly never before or since has it been dished out so copiously and so cheaply. Italian opera appeared as early as 1851, coinciding with the first macaroni factories. It immediately became a *corvee* of the *haut monde*. According to Mr. Idwal Jones, white gloves made their first appearance on the West Coast at a performance of *La Sonnambula* in 1853.[5] Grand opera became progressively more expensive and more chic until the 1890s, when it became cheaper and more vulgar, probably as a result of the revolutions going on in Central America.

The connection does not appear readily obvious but it is quite simple. Whenever the streets of an afflicted republic become too thick with angry murmuring, the president cabled a rush order to Naples for an opera company; he fed the mobs the soothing melodies of Verdi and they became quiet for a while. These operatic circuses were much cheaper than bread. The troupes usually had a long sojourn in San Francisco on the way home. Tickets then were a dollar. But it was not until North Beach had its own opera company that grand opera became unmistakably popular—at two bits a head in the Washington Square Theatre.

This was Italian opera of the unfashionable type, hot and tumultuous and fiercely erratic. It had its stars, Ismael Magagna and Luigi Poggi, Cesare Gravina and others, whose personalities and comic misadventures are described in the sprightly prose of Mr. Idwal Jones, a former dramatic critic for the *San Francisco Examiner*. In an entertaining article for the *American Mercury*, Mr. Jones remembers that Signor Poggi was "a delightful man whose inability to read music was more than recompensed by his quick wits." He relates several instances when Poggi extricated himself from hazardous *contretemps* with the utmost of *savoir-faire*. Once (as the clown in *I Pagliacci*) he discovered, as he was about to make the fatal thrust, that he had forgotten his poniard. So he clutched his windpipe and roared passionately all over the stage like a wounded bull until he dropped. Another time, as the bandit chieftain in *Fra Diavolo*, he was about to be shot but the *carabiniere* missed fire. The gallery jeered, the *carabiniere*, cursing, leveled his gun and again—silence. Poggi, unruffled, raised his arms high, yelled "BOOM!"—and toppled with a resounding crash that roused the patrons to the heights of enthusiasm.

Another quaint character was Magagna, "*Il fenomenal tenore Messicana*," who had great difficulty in making his appearances on time because of his devotion to Morpheus. He was very proficient in this activity, often sleeping 20 hours at a time without the slightest effort. On the stage he had a tremendous dignity. Tells Mr. Jones:

> A quarter was a pathetically small sum to pay for the privilege of witnessing human dignity at its apotheosis in Magagna as Don Jose. It was dented, only once, when a child in its mother's arms began to wail in the midst of Magagna's set-piece. The audience hissed at the interruption, and the sounds reached the tenor's ears. He paled, drew himself up, and addressed the house thus:
>
> "*Signori e Signore*: I have sung the world over, from La Scala to Buenos Aires. I have been cheered in London, and the critics—si, the highest critics—of Madrid have deigned to praise me. I have been applauded in Berlin and Belgrade"—tears rolled down the grease paint—"but this is the first time I have been accorded the incivility of a hissing."
>
> The audience got up and shouted, "No, No, Ismael—See, we applaud! *Ha cantato bene!*" Thus appeased Magagna made a profound bow, did the aria all over again, and retired to the cellar to sleep.

Behind this remarkable venture in popular opera was the dynamic, modest, little impresario, Camillo Porreco, who acted as manager, publicity agent, ticket seller, and occasionally sang as an amateur in the chorus. It is somewhere said that "opera in San Francisco is like spaghetti without cheese"; it was undoubtedly Porreca who said it.

38. "SING FOR THEIR SUPPER"

The bottle of wine served between the acts in the Green Room was the pay of the amateurs in the chorus. It would have been as impossible as the cheeseless spaghetti were it not for the platter of crisp, aromatic fennel that came with it. For it is the strange property of this herb that one bite of it will make week-old claret taste like cob-webbed Montreux.

The directory of the company, Maestro August Serantoni, received a little higher recompense, but still his wage was less than nominal. He got a dollar a night, which was also the pay of the professional members of the chorus. Maestro Serantoni is also a little man but he is more self-effacing than Porreca; nevertheless, he was not only the director but the whole orchestra of the company, playing the piano with one hand and directing with the other.

Making allowances for Mr. Jones' little flights into fancy (according to Porreca, Serantoni often received as much as two or three dollars a night) it is delightful to recapture the spirit of this brief period in San Francisco when opera was enjoyed for itself and not as a fetish; when there was opera because people loved to hear it and people loved to sing it. There was no clamor for funds to support million dollar opera houses and million dollar stars; there was no problem of finances, because there were no finances.

"Maestro," said a gushing American admirer to Serantoni one night, "I am glad you have only the piano. We can hear the voices all the better."

"In that case," he gallantly replied, "we shall dispense with the piano, so you can hear even better. Anyway, the installment collectors will be around after the show."

For a time there was a tremendous, gay spontaneity. Just as in 1910 the Maoris had brought drama to its peak in North Beach, Serantoni and Porreca brought genuinely popular opera to Washington Square.

39. THE MEXICAN INVASION

For some time the Italian theatre had been declining—not only legitimate drama but even the more popular genres of operetta, farce and variety. For the fickle public, craving novelty, there was a scarcity of new faces and voices in 1922. The Spanish theatre was flourishing in North Beach. The Signora Impresario had for the moment transferred her interest to the Mexicans, and the Italian theatre, without her support, was collapsing. She had installed the Compañia de Comedias y Variedades Internacionales in the Liberty Theatre, now renamed the Teatro Crescent. She brought to San Francisco the famous Mexican comedian, Romualo Tirado, and his company.

Signora Alessandro had spent several months in Mexico, searching for a company she could bring to San Francisco. Now, with the Spanish situation taken care of for a time, she could turn her attention to her famished Italian public. The Italians were indeed in a sorry plight; they had lost both their theatres to the Mexicans and the Americans, and the public was weary of the old familiar actors. Signora Alessandro decided on a resolute step; she would journey eastward, and, if necessary, to Italy, to satisfy the demands of her public. Nothing was too good for North Beach. But before she went, a *Grande Serata Straordinaria* was held for her at the Crescent Theatre. It was a mixed performance: Tirado's Spanish company performed in a comedy sketch; there was an Argentine tango, a marimba band, and other variety numbers; Signora Caranza sang several popular Italian songs; and Signora Alessandro herself played the part of the mother, Carmela, in a Neapolitan dramatic sketch, *Nu Guaglione è Malavita*.

40. THE ALESSANDRO EDEN THEATRE

On her return Antonietta Pisanelli Alessandro set about finding a permanent theatre building to house the Italian theatre. The years had not impaired the Neapolitan lady's finesse in intrigue. On Green Street she discovered a little Protestant church that was obviously not prospering and she persuaded the church people that it would be better for them if she took it over. So the Signora Impresario leased the building for a song and set about remodeling the interior. She borrowed money here, borrowed money there, rented the ground floor out as a moving picture theatre, and finally, in July 1924, she opened the new Little Italian Theatre, the Teatro Italiano di Varietà. It was familiarly known as the Teatro Alessandro Eden; the years had not changed the Signora's fondness for personal display.

This theatre, too, was destined to fall out of Italian hands; when their grip relaxed for a moment it fell to a third-rate stock company which put on *Easy for Zee Zee*, and other risqué shows, completely destroying its reputation as a family theatre. Subsequently it became the Green Street Theatre, which, with façade still unchanged, housed the Theatre Union and its left-wing dramas; but it was no longer an Italian playhouse. The Italian theatre, at that point, was gone from North Beach.

But on June 10, 1924 things looked very promising for the Italian theatre. On that date, according to *L'Italia*, the Italian colony was offered the opportunity to see, examine and admire "*l'elegantissimo ed italianissimo teatro*," for flags and banners were strewn about liberally and the decorations were in the Italian colors. A "select public" filled the seats, whose arms could readily be transformed into little tables at which one might eat ice cream or cake, or sip coffee (this was during Prohibition). The commercially-adept Signora Alessandro had not forgotten the lucrative adventure of the Circolo Famigliare Pisanelli; she was ever mindful of the value of *café-chantants*, programs, curtains, fans, and other side-enterprises.

41. THE GENIUS OF LA ALESSANDRO AGAIN

The program was typical of the *café-chantant* motif: an assortment of young ladies and young gentlemen sang various songs, popular and classical. Then an animated Spanish lady, Maria Miceli, sang several Aragonese numbers, accompanied on the piano by the Maestro G. Miceli. next two Italian girls played violins. But the greatest success of the evening was the eight-year-old Totò Cecchini in the comedy with transformation, *Il Piccolo Demonietto (The Little Devil)*. Little Totò was commended for his poise on the stage, his clarity of diction, and his easy handling of costume and mood changes. A brilliant future was predicted for him. The public must have thought so too because they applauded him with frenzy; in the applause the perspicacious critic also discovered elements of "sincere emotion." Cecchini père supported his son capably in the sketch; he was also good in the *scherzo comico* with his wife, the Signora Teresa Cecchini-Aguglia. With the Cecchini family thus disposing of the dramatic branch of the entertainment the inaugural program came to an end.

Yet Signora Alessandro must have thought that the inauguration of the Teatro Alessandro Eden was lacking in the brilliant and the spectacular. For on October 3, somewhat belatedly, she had the Nuova Teatro Italiano di Varietà officially baptized by no less a personage than the noted tenor, Tito Schipa, who happened to be in town at the time. The impressive ceremony was preceded by a *Spettacolo di Gala* in which participated such artists as: Enrico Martinelli, Florence Ringo, Nona Campbell, Maria Miceli, Guido Trento, the Parisi couple, and the Minciottis, husband and wife.

At this time the ingenious Signora Impresario was discovering a new method of advertising. A member of the prolific Aguglia family, Gigi Aguglia, was at the Alessandro Eden with his operetta troupe, La Compagnia dei Sette; they were giving operettas every night. And every day Signora Alessandro circulated little handbills advertising the performance with such statements as "Two hours of continuous entertainment," and pungent remarks as "*Il riso fa buon sangue*" (Laughter brings health). There was also a humorous drawing, such as one finds among the caricatures of the Italian newspapers, with dialogue. One program displays a rather chic flapper, accompanied by a dog who is accosted by a little, shrivelled, ragged old woman. The mother, for such she appears to be, is vexed. This is a translation of the dialogue:

> The Mother: Where are you going with that little dog? Don't you know you are making a hideous appearance?

The Daughter: Mama! But I have no other diversion!

The Mother: Well, if it is a question of diversion, this evening I will take you to see *Casta Susanna* at the Alessandro Eden and I am sure that you will be content....

It is not a very funny joke, but then neither are comic strips that exhibit the energetic hero in various melodramatic adventures always climaxed by a stirring tribute to a popular breakfast food. It is a sly means of luring the unwary victim into the trap; and Signora Alessandro deserves some credit for having anticipated the big-time advertising agencies by several years.

And the Signora Impresario could also put out programs that were less crude. For the *Serata di Gala* in behalf of the monument to Dante she distributed rather handsome souvenir programs in the form of little booklets, with bronze-colored covers ornamented by the famous medallion portrait of Dante, and with a rhetorical tribute to the great poet by Giovanni Pascoli, entitled "*Il Fuoco Eterno d'Italia*" ("The Eternal Fire of Italy"). The program also included the inevitable portrait of Signora Alessandro slightly smaller in size than that of Dante and also those of the principal members of the Alessandro company: Guido Trento, Signor and Signora Minciotti, Enrico Martinelli, Giuseppe Miceli, and Santuzza and Renzo Todini. The company appeared in a series of songs and instrumental solos; this was followed by a one-act play, *Illusi* by Cesari and *Gianciotto*, a comedy by Borg. There were long intermissions between the acts, during which the audience could study very closely the fifty or more little advertisements in the booklet.

The public was invited to contribute to the patriotic cause which was under the auspices of the North Beach Promotion Association. Whether or not the *Serata di Gala* was a success is difficult to ascertain; at any rate a monument to Dante has yet to be erected in North Beach.

Soon, however, the public was distracted from the patriotic cause. Signora Alessandro had found a new attraction for the Alessandro Eden, an old favorite. In 1925 Alfredo Aratoli returned in glory to North Beach; Stenterello had come to say "*Addio*" to his San Francisco friends.

42. THE LAST OF STENTERELLO

As if aware that this was his swan song, Stenterello rose to unusual heroic heights. He was "*Marinaio per forza ed uccisor di briganti*" ("Sailor in spite of himself and killer of bandits"); he was a "Faithful friend and ambitious warrior"; he was a "Fruit-seller and savior of his country." He took part in famous melodramas by Bargiacchi: *Veneranda Porto ovvero il Delitto di Tommaso Centenari*, in which Stenterello appeared as "water carrier, ridiculous witness and defender of innocence"; *The Victim of Tevere, or Faith, Hope and Charity*, featuring the agile and ubiquitous Stenterello as "beggar, vendor of statuettes, traveling salesman, condemned to death by the court of Rome." But somehow the wily Stenterello managed to escape his fate and was next seen as a "dealer in musical instruments and piano mover" in the very brassy-sounding drama of *La Società Tromboni, Bombardini e Corni*.

Besides its Stenterello, the Città di Firenze Company also had an operatic division directed by Luigi Badolati. On the very first night of the season, May 11, 1925, some of the members supplemented the *Grandiosa Stenterellata* with music: Maria Garuffi sang a Florentine love song, Stella Bruno from Rome sang a Neapolitan song, Badolati sang an operatic aria. The next evening the company put on the popular operetta of student life in Turin, *Addio Giovanezza*. This was followed a few days later by a new operetta from Italy, *His Majesty the Dollar*. In the succeeding weeks they sang many other operettas, new and old, including many of American origin. Some of the favorites were *Acqua Chieta, The Chaste Susanna, The Count of Luxembourg, The Slipper Lost in the Snow, La Petite Chocolatière*.

In reality, Stenterello was running a losing race for popular favor with the operetta. As the City of Florence Company continued to play nightly at the Alessandro Eden Theatre, it was felt more and more that Stenterello was becoming an anachronism. Yet Aratoli, with a touching fidelity to tradition, continued to draw on the inexhaustible sources of the Stenterello repertoire: the variety comedies, the melodramas, the farces, in which Stenterello appeared; these were used to fill out an evening mainly devoted to operetta. For three years, an unprecedented record, the Città di Firenze Company played in the Alessandro Eden, changing the program every night, presenting variety, grand opera, melodrama, operetta, comedy and Stenterellate.

43. THE MINCIOTTIS

In the meantime, every night, at the Liberty and sometimes at the Washington Square, the Minciottis were also giving a varied program of stock drama, variety, comedy and operetta. Both companies were rather loosely organized and there was a constant interchange of actors. Thus, on December 19, 1925, Ester and Silvio Minciotti played the protagonists of *Giulietta e Romeo*; in the cast were Scarpa and Tricoli. The following evening, Sardou's popular *Tosca* was given, together with a vocal concert by Stella Bruno and Badolati of the Città di Firenze Company; Aratoli himself appeared later in the evening in a Stenterello farce. On January 23, *I Tre Moschetieri*, an adaptation by Altavilla from the Dumas novel was given, with the tenor Badolati in the role of D'Artagnan. With a delightful facility the actors leaped from one company to another, slipped from operetta to melodrama, and from farce to tragedy. They were true Italian actors.

On January 26, 1926 the Minciotti Company produced *The Count of Monte Cristo*; on the 30th they put on another Dumas melodrama, *A Night at Florence, or, the Guelfs and the Ghibellines*. They were exceedingly partial to the Dumas genre of historical-romantic melodrama. In other ways the Minciotti season rolled back time to the Maori season of 1910. They gave the standard works of the European stock theatre; among others, such venerable war horses as *Otello*, *Morte Civile*, *Francsca da Rimini*, and *Fèdora*.

But occasionally a new work would be presented. The romantic opera, *La Monaca Bianca*, was a great success, already made familiar to cinema audiences as *The White Sister*. Ester Minciotti was the protagonist of this sad drama of sacrifice and renunciation, reprising Lillian Gish's famous role. Opposite her was her husband, Silvio Minciotti; also in the cast were Ernestina, their eldest daughter; Luigi Badolati, Mario Scarpa, and Stella Bruno of the Città di Firenze Company. This opera in three acts and a prologue, by Clemente Gigli, was of the spectacle genre, so dear to Italian hearts. It had everything in it from an impressive ceremony in which the heroine takes the sacred vows of sisterhood to a sensational scene in which Vesuvius boils over and the panic-stricken peasantry run wildly all over the stage as the orchestra plays suitable seismographic music. There was passion, love, jealousy, grief, and music: Ave Marias, love duets, volcanic music.

La Monaca Bianca was a hit; in fact so successful was the first performance at the Liberty Theatre that it had to be repeated, an unusual event in the Italian theatre, where programs were regularly changed nightly.

The two companies now playing in North Beach willingly exchanged performers. Both were small and often it was necessary to borrow actors and singers from one another for special occasions. Not only were the casts variable, but there was even a constant shifting from one theatre to another. In February the Minciottis were playing at the Alessandro Eden Theatre. On Monday, February 16, they repeated another favorite, *La Morte Civile*. This was the beginning of a typical week of the Minciotti season: on Tuesday they gave *Pia dei Tolomei* with Stenterello; on Wednesday two comedies—*Piedigrotta 1925* and *Er Fatacio*; on Thursday a four-act drama, *Beppe Melacine*; on Friday a musical revue, *La Figlia della Strada (The Girl of the Street)*; on Saturday a comedy, *Il Biricchino di Parigi (The Gamin of Paris)*, starring Ester Minciotti; on Sunday a two-act operetta, *Il Duca Giardiniere*; on Monday they celebrated the holiday, Washington's Birthday, with a *Spettacoli di Gala*.

During the years 1925-28 the two companies played in North Beach giving every variety of performance known to the theatre, filling the houses virtually every night—switching from the Alessandro Eden Theatre to the Liberty and then to the Washington Square Theatre when a larger house was needed for more lavish spectacles. Next to the bright afternoon of the Maori season of 1910-12, the season of the Aratolis-Minciottis of 1925-28 was the richest period—the glowing twilight—of the Italian theatre in San Francisco.

44. THE SCHISM

By 1928 the Italian theatre had entered upon a rapid decline. Back in April 1925, at the Alessandro Eden, Signora Alessandro had staged a *Spettacolo di Gala* to celebrate the twentieth anniversary of the Italian theatre in San Francisco. There was a special performance of vocal and instrumental music; the one-act drama, *Cavalleria Rusticana* and the farce, *Prestami tua Moglie per Dieci Minuti* were revived for the occasion, performed just as they had been given at the Teatro Apollo on April 9, 1905, with as many of the original actors as were available. It was the last *Spettacolo di Gala* given for the Signora Impresario—a final gesture. For the Italian theatre was dying and the Signora Impresario who had almost single-handedly supported it through its many vicissitudes, was abandoning it to its fate. The fresh streams of immigration on which the theatre had relied had dried up; the immigration laws of 1922 were decimating the public of the Italian theatre. The Americanization—or should we say, de-Italianization—process was withering the Italian theatre. Moving pictures, also, were contributing to the general dissolution. For a time it looked as if the Italian theatre was ready for the tomb. Signora Alessandro's *Spettacolo di Gala* resembled a commemoration rather than a celebration.

After a dismal lapse, however, things began to improve. Radio was becoming popular and "Italian hours" were giving employment to some of the idle actors. The medium was instrumental, to a large extent, in preserving Italian language and drama; at least it gave people an opportunity to hear advertising announcements in Italian and some scattered fragments of Italian dialogue.

In 1929 Frank Puglia, who had come to San Francisco with the Compagnia dei Sette of Gigi Aguglia, and was now on the radio, organized his own company and played a moderately successful season of stock at the Washington Square Theatre. In 1931 Primo Brunetti, who had been Mimi Aguglia's leading man in 1914 and later toured America with her company, arrived in San Francisco. He formed a company with R. Bernardini, Seragnoli, and Scarpa; together they performed many of the Italian classics which were part of the Aguglia repertoire, such as *La Nemica*.

In 1932 Brunetti rejoined Mimi Aguglia at the Washington Square (renamed the Milano). But even with the prestige of l'Aguglia, the Italian theatre could not operate on its traditional basis, changing programs every night. Performances were now given on the average of once a month. Under the influence of Mimi Aguglia the dying Italian theatre was transfused with new blood and directed into another channel. The career of Mimi Aguglia in San Francisco covers the transition of the popular theatre into a subsidized "Art Theatre with a Purpose." This phase of the history of the Italian theatre in San Francisco is given in the specially detailed section, Part II, and suggests one possible solution for the survival of the foreign language theatre in America today.

PART II

IL TEATRO ITALIANO

Carlo Tricoli

1. THE ITALIAN THEATRE

In Italy the stage was very much a product of long-standing tradition, and the actors were generally descendants of sixteenth- and seventeenth-century puppet players, circus clowns, and the Pulcinella and Arlecchino of the Commedia dell'Arte. A typical example are the Lupinos, an ancient family of puppet players, who first migrated to England during the reign of James I, and who have included in their history actors, dancers and acrobats. The contemporary representatives of the family include the comedian George Lupino (1853-1932), his actor-playwright-producer son Stanley (1895-1942), and Stanley's daughter, Ida Lupino, the talented and popular Hollywood actress who began her career on the London stage.

The Teatro Italiano of San Francisco illustrates remarkably well how the Italian theatre became the monopoly of a few substantial families, and how persistently acting ran in the blood. Vladimiro Brunetti and Argentina Ferraù, an energetic and likeable young couple, pre-sided over the destinies of the Teatro Italiano. With them, from time to time, were associated Primo Brunetti and Vincenzo Ferraù—leading man and artistic director—and their respective fathers. The Brunettis, originating in Rome and Bologna, had acted in Italy for over two hundred years, and Primo Brunetti was the cousin of the great Sicilian actress, Tina di Lorenzo. Vencenzo Ferraù was the husband of Mimi Aguglia, also a cousin of Tina di Lorenzo. And, to complicate matters more completely, it may be mentioned that Argentina Ferraù was the wife of Vladimiro Brunetti!

Out of this involved inheritance arose a hereditary facility and a disinterested zeal in the theatre. The companies they headed were generally of professional ability, but, in the strictest sense of the word, they were amateurs, acting only because it was in their blood—and because it was their passion.

The Teatro Italiano was a "Theatre of Art"; it was concerned with the best in the field of the modern Italian theatre. Pirandello and d'Annunzio were favorite sources. In the last few seasons they produced works solely by Italian authors, and their productions were selected primarily for their value as examples of Italian art and culture.

They represented the modern Italians almost exclusively. The work of the Teatro Italiano could be compared with that of Andre Ferrier's Théâtre d'Art Français. The example of Ferrier's success undoubtedly stimulated the organization of the permanent Italian theatre. The Italian newspapers were deeply interested in Ferrier's experiment, and, on the occasion of the opening of the second season of the Teatro Italiano, *L'Italia* became almost oratorical in its appeal to its countrymen's sense of pride and honor:

> The persistence of one man and the co-operation of a colony have given to San Francisco a permanent legitimate theatre, truly worthy of praise. This man is Andre Ferrier; this colony is the French....Why then is it not possible for our compatriots [the Italians] to create a real institution of prose in San Francisco, that can be worthy of such a name, both by its high cultural aim and the earnestness of the organization?[6]

The Teatro Italiano had been earnestly contemplating this objective. It had dutifully observed Mussolini's decrees about disseminating Italian propaganda through Italian art—the production of the best Italian works for the diffusion of the Italian language—for "*Il teatro e la scuola della vita, la migliore cattedra da cui si puo imparare il nostro dolce idioma.*" ("*The theatre is the school of life, the best place where our beautiful language can be learned.*")

Yet the Teatro Italiano was by no means a popular Italian institution; it was supported mainly by a few Americans and the most influential of the Italian societies: the Dante Alighieri Society, the Italy-America Society, the Cenacolo Club, the Figli d'Italia, and the Vittoria Colonna. No concessions were made to the masses. Thus the Teatro Italiano fell short of its stated purpose of bringing the theatre in contact with the people, "in educating the people to love the theatre."

Yet it had many illustrious achievements to its credit; it brought to San Francisco for the first time Pirrandello's *Six Characters in Search of an Author,* and it permitted San Francisco to enjoy, for two successive seasons, the fascinating art of the "*tragica moderna*" Mimi Aguglia—called by Italian critics the successor to Ristori and Duse.

2. MIMI AGUGLIA

It is not difficult to understand the extraordinary career of Mimi Aguglia in the light of a romantic heredity and a remarkable birth. In traditional style her mother, the beautiful Contessa di Lorenzo of Palermo, had defied a noble family and eloped with a base-born and penniless student of the seminary. They had met at an amateur performance held in a church where the young countess played the ingénue and the young candidate for the priesthood was its musical director. Later, when all other practical solutions to a livelihood failed, the couple returned to the theatre.

They played in various towns in Sicily; Signora Aguglia learned how to act and in due time became a member of Salvini's company. Signor Aguglia, musically inclined, but without any music to direct, laboriously made copies of the scripts and acted as prompter of the company; and always in his spare time, with characteristic Sicilian jealousy, he maintained constant and passionate vigilance over his wife's comings and goings.

In the course of time Signora Aguglia became an expectant mother, but still her husband would not let her out of his sight, and the docile wife had to accompany her husband to the theatre every night.

One evening, in the midst of a performance of *Otello*, the leading lady suddenly took it into her head to quarrel with the manager and rushed off with a member of the audience. Here was Othello but no Desdemona. The manager was frantic. Finally he spotted Signora Aguglia sitting quietly in a corner knitting. He requested she go on. She protested; she was in no condition to do so. The manager became more and more insistent and then violent. He summoned Aguglia and threatened to fire them both at once. Signor Aguglia glanced meaningfully at his wife—and she dutifully took to the stage.

Eventually the last act began with the terrible and vindictive Othello strangling Desdemona in her immaculate bed. The audience was delighted by the lady's realistic moaning. Her cries became more and more persistent until Othello, perturbed, muttered to her to lie still and die quietly—then the moaning ceased.

Othello completed his scene by consummating the fearful tragedy. The curtain fell. Suddenly from Desdemona's death bed came the sharp cry of an infant. The curtain did not rise again that evening. Mimi Aguglia had made her first appearance...literally!

It was sometime in the 1890s that Mimi Aguglia thus made her debut in Desdemona's boudoir. She spent the rest of her life on the stage, everywhere: Sicily, Italy, France, England, Spain, Mexico, South America, Central America,

New York, Hollywood, San Francisco; but she was solely and completely a Sicilian actress, all nerves and passion, a volcano—full of the fire of her native Sicily.

By the age of twelve Mimi was supporting her father and a covey of brothers and sisters, all potential actors and actresses. The intense emotionalism of her acting had begun to arouse excitement in critical circles throughout Italy. The author, Edmond de Amicis, saw her perform in *Malia* and ran to the poet, Gabriele d'Annunzio, raving about the depth and richness of the child's artistry, and her ability to convey, with almost clinical precision, the terrible nuances of hysteria and madness.

3. L'AGUGLIA AND D'ANNUNZIO

D'Annunzio went to Sicily to see this new phenomenon in action. He did not visit her in the crowded dressing room after the performance, preferring to wait and greet her alone.

The two authors sat quietly in the empty theatre. A frail little girl in Sicilian peasant costume, sauntered cheerfully toward them from the direction of the dressing room, eating an apple. She grinned at D'Annunzio and sat down. D'Annunzio looked at her and frowned.

"I wish to see Signorina Aguglia," he said.

"*Si*, I am Signorina Aguglia," replied the child, taking another bite.

The poet thinking, "A little sister," persisted: "But I wish to see *Mimi* Aguglia."

"*Ma si*," she said, "I *am* Mimi Aguglia, the great actress."

"Hm," said the poet, "an impudent brat." And as she continued to insist, with disconcerting assurance, that she was indeed Mimi Aguglia, he offered to spank her. The little girl burst into tears and rushed off.

In a moment she was back, dragging Giovanni Grasso, the *capo comico*, by the hand. "Tell them I am Mimi Aguglia," she demanded. And the poet fell to his knees, kissing her hand and begging forgiveness for not having recognized in this puny child the terrible demoness of Malia.[7]

Gabriele d'Annunzio was so impressed with her performances that he wrote the play, *La Figlia di Jorio*, specifically for her, and it was this play that eventually made Mimi Aguglia famous throughout Italy and all of Europe. Restraint had no part in the Italian theatre of the time—neither in acting nor in criticism. The first Sicilian performance of *La Figlia di Jorio* brought an exalted burst of rhapsodic prose from the critic, Alessandro Varaldo. A translation of a fragment of his critique feebly suggests his rapturous enthusiasm:

> One cannot attain a higher peak, climb as Mimi Aguglia does, with more strength, greatness, genius. This actress cannot be measured by the common scale, she soars like the eagle, escapes us like a vision of a dream or incantation: she is the mistress of her soul, binds it, chains it, forcing her will to an amazing dualism. I see her in the first act of the drama, clinging to the hospitable hearth, shivering with a superhuman terror: she trembles and bursts into flames: with the cat-like leaping of a panther, at times her instinct incites her, then suddenly despair

overcomes her; and she drags herself along the floor, cowering, stretching out her hands and weeping, sobbing with a painful fury of impotence and crawling on the ground with hoarse accents of madness, of terror, of delirium....

Linguistic moderation was unknown to the exuberant Italian critic. In reading the advertisements of Italian performances one remarks upon the peculiar Italian indulgence in emotional sprees. A play is advertised as *"Tre atti d'intensa emozione attraverso la gamma di tutte le passioni umane"* ("Three acts of intense emotion traversing the gamut of all human passions")—which is certainly getting your money's worth, for a 25-cent gallery seat.

Mimi's precocity manifested itself in other ways. The director, Vincenzo Ferraù, a man twenty years her elder, was also with the company of Giovanni Grasso. Her father, Signor Aguglia, had by now wisely transferred his vigilance from mother to daughter. When Mimi was off the stage he stationed himself in front of her dressing room; at night he bolted the door of her bedchamber, all to no avail. A fellow actor helped to confound the jealous father by carrying notes between the two lovers. Predictably, Mimi, one evening, climbed out of a small window, down a long ladder, and was spirited off to a nearby church by Ferraù. She was fifteen years old.

4. EUROPEAN TRIUMPHS

Leaving Sicily with the company of Giovanni Grasso, Mimi Aguglia played throughout Italy where her fame had preceded her. Paris claimed her next, then London, where she gave a special command performance of *La Figlia di Jorio* before the entire royal family of Edward VII. Their attendance, it was said, defied tradition, and for the first time in history left the British throne unguarded.

An Italian critic reported that the staid population of the Eng-lish metropolis was overwhelmed as if by a tremendous charge of lightning—"*colpita come sotto una scarica torrenziale d'elettricità.*" London critic Walkley's style is less subjective than that of Varaldo—more coldly analytical—but he, too, exclaimed in wonder at the wild, delirious quality of Mimi Aguglia's acting:

> We have called Mimi Aguglia's acting hysterico-epileptic, and now, as before, her acting seems to be not a matter of deliberate volition, still less of reasoned calculation, but rather the case of a patient in convulsions....Even now as we write, we can still see this small, rather squat, gypsy-looking woman, with the big circles around the eyes, and the tangle of blue-black hair, cowering in the corner of the Shaftesbury stage, a hunted animal, quivering, sputtering, gasping with terror.[8]

L'Aguglia, "The Actress of a Thousand Faces," had a magnificent vitality and an extraordinary versatility. For many years she travelled constantly all over Europe and America. She played in everything, from the most austere tragedy, to the sprightliest comedy and she performed in four languages—Italian, French, Spanish and English. Her *Salomé* (by Oscar Wilde) presented both in Italian and English, was one of her greatest triumphs—and indeed it was a part made to order for her.

Mimi Aguglia's appearances in America were especially compelling. Under the auspices of Daniel Frohman she toured the United States in 1914, playing for one month in San Francisco. Here she performed in a group of d'Annunzio's plays which included *La Figlia di Jorio*, the piece written for her. (Later *La Figlia di Jorio* was produced in English in the natural amphitheatre at Mount Tamalpais.)

5. L'AGUGLIA IN AMERICA

In July 1914 Mimi Aguglia descended upon San Francisco. She had been acclaimed in New York and Chicago, where her success had been almost as great as in Europe. Audiences had flocked to see her, composed mainly of people who did not understand Italian; but so universal was her appeal, so eloquent her gestures, facial expressions and vocal intonations that her performances had no need of translation. She reminded the critics of Duse, Réjane, and Bernhardt; and they marvelled that one so young (she was estimated variously as being between 25 and 27) could have achieved so much in her art. On the stages of Europe she had appeared in more than two hundred leading roles.

Mimi Aguglia did not disappoint her San Francisco public. She announced a week's engagement at the Cort Theatre starting on Monday, July 13th, with matinees Wednesday and Sunday at popular prices: matinees, 25 cents to $1.00; evenings, 25 cents to $1.50. Her repertoire consisted of those tragic works that were her special *forté*.

She led off on Monday with the tragedy by d'Annunzio which had brought her world fame, *La Figlia di Jorio*, playing the role she had created, that of the terror-ridden peasant girl, Mila di Corda. This was always one of her most impressive and powerful interpretations, permitting unlimited scope to her realistic acting. Without a question *La Figlia di Jorio* is the most theatrical of all of d'Annunzio's tragedies—and l'Aguglia's intense evocation of its primitive passions and superstitions has at times almost intolerably exacerbated the nerves of Anglo-Saxon audiences.

The Italians in the audience at the Cort Theatre, at any rate, showed unanimous and enthusiastic response to Mimi Aguglia's acting. They made up in noisy approbation what they lacked in numbers, and were wildly extravagant with their shouts of *"Bravo"* and *"Bravissimo."* *L'Italia* of July 14, 1914 comments on the fine artistic and patriotic zeal of the audience, noting with approval the clamorous and fervent demonstrations at the end of the tragedy. In reviewing the performance, *L'Italia* managed to add a few extra superlatives to toss upon the rest of the company, finding in the leading man, Sterni, an *"artista coscienzioso e correttissimo"* ("a most conscientious and correct artist")—which may indeed be considered faint praise after the magnificent encomia lavished upon Mimi Aguglia.

Tuesday evening found Mimi Aguglia living up to her reputation for versatility in the title role of Sardou's popular drama *Fèdora*. As the imperious and cruel Russian princess in this play of revolutionary intrigue she had an altogether different role from that of the wretched outcast of d'Annunzio's tragedy. *Fèdora* was originally written for Sarah Bernhardt. Brought to America in 1883, it gave

Fanny Davenport a great triumph. Now there was an opportunity to compare Mimi Aguglia's interpretation with the others.

At the Wednesday matinee she repeated *La Figlia di Jorio*, and for the evening performance gave another drama by Sardou in which she was the pathetic protagonist of *Odette*. The plays of Sardou were popular with the Italian public because they were not only well-constructed, substantial dramas, and simply motivated—but they were filled with the conventional ingredients of *l'amore, la passione, la gelosia, la vendetta, e la morte* (love, passion, jealousy, revenge, and death.)

Aguglia returned to the Italian authors with *La Cena delle Beffe* on Thursday night. This verse-tragedy by Sam Benelli, rhetorically depicting the gaudy and sombre Florence of the Medicis, is a welcome vehicle for actors of the florid school. The role of the hero, Giannetto (generally played by a woman), has been performed by Bernhardt and Tina di Lorenzo, and its tormented psychology gave full play to the resources of Mimi Aguglia. The austere passion and cruelty of *La Cena delle Beffe*, "*il poema dell'odio e della vendetta*," was a splendid vehicle for a Sicilian. (Known as *The Jest* in English, it was later performed by the Barrymore family in 1919.)

Mimi Aguglia was "*grande nello scherzo, nell'ira et nell vendetta*"—and she was admittedly also great in "*amore*." On Friday night at the Cort Theatre she proved it, matching her art with that of Bernhardt, "*du voix d'or*," and Duse "*dei belli mani*." Was she not Aguglia, "*dei mille faccie*?" On Friday night Aguglia became *La Signora delle Camelie*—*La Dame aux Camélias, Camille*, Marguerite Gautier, Violetta. Sarah Bernhardt had sat in the audience while Eleonora Duse played *La Dame aux Camélias* in Paris, and had then rushed backstage to call Duse's performance better than her own. What in turn would Duse have said of Aguglia's *Camille*? Knowing l'Aguglia's talents, and in particular her extraordinary capacity for on-stage suffering, we can speculate on her opinion.

On Saturday night L'Aguglia next turned to a tragedy of her own Sicily, to Luigi Capuana's *Malia*. In Sicily the young Mimi Aguglia had so absorbed the part of the violent, hysterical heroine, had so studied all the degrees of delirium and madness, that the celebrated psychiatrist, Lombroso, watching her perform, could describe her as: "a pathological phenomenon, to be able to simulate madness with such exactitude."[9]

At a Sunday matinee Aguglia gave another performance of *La Dame aux Camélias*, and for the evening chose to play in another of d'Annunzio's tragedies, *La Fiaccola sotto il Moggio* (*The Hidden Torch*)—this one dealing not with Sicilian peasants, but with the pastoral people of the Abruzzi; this closed her week at the Cort.

6. SECOND WEEK AT THE CORT

The San Francisco public, however, would not let her go. Despite the general unfamiliarity with the language, despite the strangeness of the Italian dramas, she was playing to crowded houses. The critic of the *Chronicle* said (on July 19, 1914):

> She is quite as remarkable an actress as San Francisco has ever known...so forthright is the method of Aguglia that she has attracted many English-speaking people to the Cort as well as her own country folk....Her wonderful expressive face and gestures and voice intonation carry the play's meaning over the footlights when mere words are not understood....Aguglia's leading man, Sterni, has made a distinct impression on Cort audiences, and the company as a whole is admirable. The simplicity of their method is noteworthy, and many American actors could learn much from these mummers from over the sea....

So clamorous was the public demand that Mimi Aguglia offered to play another week at the Cort. She selected a different repertoire—a group of plays more familiar to the American public; not only were there the usual d'Annunzio and Sardou, but also Sudermann and Bernstein and Oscar Wilde.

First, on Monday evening, was Sudermann's *Magda*. This great modern drama had had great popularity on all the European stages; in playing the title role Mimi Aguglia was adding her name to the imposing list of such interpreters as Modjeska, Bernhardt, Duse, and Mrs. Patrick Campbell.

The protean l'Aguglia played the next evening in *Il Ladro*, the Italian version of Henry Bernstein's powerful psychological drama, *Le Voleur* (*The Thief*), which had been given here in English by Margaret Illington, a native of San Francisco.

For her Wednesday matinee Aguglia repeated *Magda*, and for the evening performance played in *Ferro* (*Iron*), d'Annunzio's last tragedy.

On Thursday, Mimi Aguglia became *Salomé*, one of her greatest roles, in English as well as in Italian. The baroque, heavily ornate emotional quality of Oscar Wilde's lush tragedy in verse is well-suited to Mimi Aguglia's florid genius. Because of her successful interpretation, her views on the character are interesting. In an interview recorded by the *Chronicle* of July 19, 1914, she is quoted as saying:

> I hate it, *Salomé*. It is a terrible character, detestable in every respect, but it gives me great acting opportunities and that is why I play it, for the sake of art. If an artist would portray the horrors of a sick, decadent soul, the evil fruits of sin, one must act such roles. Happy, healthy persons do not suffer; they do not have misfortunes; they live and die in peace and contentment, and the tragedienne has no business with them. Her mission is to show what happens when humanity goes astray and pays the penalty. It is a great work and one that is worthy of genius. There is always more to be learned from suffering than from happiness.

This intelligent comment is significant; it shows that Mimi Aguglia possessed the gift of analysis, penetration into character, and an accurate knowledge of motives, the solid foundation upon which are built the inspired interpretations of great artists.

Friday evening was a special night in several respects. First, it was set aside as an evening in honor of the actress, a night during which the American public and the Italian colony would pay tribute to the artistry of Mimi Aguglia. Second, l'Aguglia chose to play in a comedy unknown to America, but which had been performed 200 times in Paris; this was the brilliant comedy of Croisset and Waliffe, *Une Américaine à Paris*. Here the great tragedienne proved that she could also be a fresh and vigorous comedienne.

She had given an indication of her comic flair in *Cavallerizza*, a short one-act comedy which followed Oscar Wilde's rhetorical tragedy. For her final matinee, on Saturday, she repeated *Salomé* and *Cavallerizza*, and closed the season with an evening performance of *Il Padrone delle Ferriere*—the Italian version of Georges Ohnet's internationally popular drama, *Le Maître de Forges* (*The Iron Master*).

The closing of her season with *Il Padrone delle Ferriere* had significance. It revealed that the great Italian tragedienne, while in San Francisco, had been trying to appeal to a wide diversity of tastes, selecting her repertoire mainly from popular European successes. Of the fourteen plays in which she performed during her two weeks at the Cort, only *six* were by Italian authors and as many from the French. Meanwhile, *L'Italia* had been steadily exhorting the Italian public to attend the Cort Theatre, "*in nome dell'arte a del patriottismo.*"

Perhaps Mimi Aguglia felt she had not, as an Italian artist and representative of Italy, fulfilled her duty to her compatriots. At any rate she set about repairing the omission by bringing the mountain to Mohammed. At the conclusion of her season at the Cort Theatre she announced a special group of performances to be given for the Italian public at the Washington Square Theatre in the heart of the Italian quarter.

7. AT WASHINGTON SQUARE

From August 3rd to 9th, Mimi Aguglia and her company played to ebullient Italian audiences in plays that are generally unknown to the greater international public, and are therefore closer to the popular Italian spirit. There was, of course, the usual Sardou—*Tosca* and *Madame Sans Gêne*, which had become a fixed part of the Italian repertoire; and there was the literary d'Annunzio's *Francesca da Rimini*. But there were also Giacometti's *Maria Antonietta*, Scarpetta's comedy, *Santorella*, Pietra Corda's *Messalina*, and Benelli's *L'Amore dei Tre Re*.

Mimi Aguglia's resources and energy were inexhaustible. She had played in one drama after another without rest, and, when one considers the violence and intensity with which she endowed her characterizations, together with her physical frailty, one can only marvel at her endurance. And still the public clamored for more. When she closed her season at the Washington Square Theatre they would not let her go; and she had to promise to remain several more weeks in San Francisco and to give occasional performances from time to time.

The success of Mimi Aguglia on her first visit to San Francisco had demonstrated the truth of certain assumptions that led in later years to the creation of the permanent Teatro Italiano: first, that there was an American public in San Francisco interested in fine acting, regardless of language; second, that there was also a public interested in Italian contributions to the world theatre; third, that among the Italian colony there were many who regarded the Italian theatre as a vital instrument for the preservation of their cultural heritage, of their *"Italianità."*

For nineteen years the Teatro Italiano remained in abeyance as Mimi Aguglia remained away from San Francisco, and as the popular theatre carried on in North Beach. Halfway between l'Aguglia's two visits, however, there occurred a great event in the San Francisco theatre, the most convincing proof that the public of the Italian theatre was not necessarily limited to Italian-speaking people—this major event was Eleanora Duse's brief visit to San Francisco in March 1924.

8. ELENORA DUSE

The fragile, withered old woman who refused make-up on the stage, or any other artificial aids for that matter, made her first visit to San Francisco after an absence of many years. After a brief appearance in Los Angeles, Charlie Chaplin had written:

> Her technique is so marvelously finished and complete, it ceases to be technique. She is, obviously...a very old woman; yet, there is something about her that suggests a pitiful child. I suppose this is the simplicity of her art...Bernhardt was always studied and more or less artificial. Duse is direct and terrible....[10]

The great tragedienne was now sixty-four, but the critics still wondered at the perfection of her profile, the vigor of her carriage, the eloquence of her hands. They were particularly enraptured by "the extraordinary beauty, power, flexibility and color of her voice."[11] To many her art was something entirely new, so unlike the quickened movement of American acting, but something deliberate and florid. The intense, at times painful, realism of her acting recalled to some the hysterical frenzy of Mimi Aguglia. But Duse was much more the consummate artist with a greater and more subtle wealth of expressiveness; unlike l'Aguglia the Sicilian, she was of the North and more restrained. But she was still profoundly Italian and, in the mounting horrors of *Spettri* she could be terrible, "terrible as a sibyl uttering a crushing prophecy."[12]

Spettri, the popular Italian version of Ibsen's *Ghosts*, was performed on March 10, a week after another drama of mother love, Praga's *La Porta Chiusa* (*The Closed Door*). The opening appearance brought a fashionable audience to the Casino Theatre, the usual crowd that attends opening nights of operas and horse shows. There was, however, a large number of Italians who were very noisy and made the star come out for almost two dozen curtain calls. This, according to the reporter, was one of the things that made San Francisco especially cosmopolitan that night. There were also many notables in the audience.

The largest audience, however, attended la Duse's third performance, when she gave her famous interpretation of the blind wife in *La Città Morta*. In this play she demonstrated that after almost twenty years of retirement she could repeat the triumphs of her youth, when she had inspired d'Annunzio's passion and poetry and had communicated them to the world.

La Duse bowed out of San Francisco in *Così Sia* (*May It Be So*), which had been written for her in 1921—an answer to critics who had said that on her return to the stage she would not be able to create a new character. *Così Sia*, like most *tour de forces*, is not an important drama; it was written solely to showcase the star's virtuosity. It permitted her to display, in impressively sweeping fashion, all the diverse phases of mother love, as the peasant mother, the woman of the people.

And the audience at this play was moved, just as the audiences had been moved by her other performances. To many who saw Duse on her last visit to America in 1924, it was the greatest emotional experience of their lives—in or out of the theatre. They contemplated this feeble, worn old woman and found that, on the stage and illuminated by the footlights, she was young and graceful, inexpressibly beautiful, inspired, incredibly alive. Many did not know that every performance was for her an ordeal, and that she often collapsed when the curtain came down and had to be revived for the curtain calls. San Francisco saw Eleanora Duse in March 1924; a month later this renowned artist, probably the greatest of all tragediennes, died in Pittsburgh, Pennsylvania.

9. THE RETURN OF MIMI AGUGLIA

Following her American tour, Mimi Aguglia set forth to the Latin-American countries, where she became immensely popular, performing as she did in both Spanish and Italian. She was so beloved, in fact, that, as she was winding up her tour in Buenos Aires, an admiring public insisted that Mimi remain in Argentina long enough for her baby to be born there, and that Eleonora Duse (who was expected in Buenos Aires shortly) would be its godmother. This she agreed to. In due time, Mimi's daughter was born, and, as befitted the occasion, the baptismal ceremony was performed on the stage of the Opera House, the Odéon, with La Duse in attendance. Since the infant was a girl, she was appropriately christened "Argentina."

Then, after all her other triumphs, Mimi Aguglia suddenly discovered that she possessed a voice, an exceptional singing voice. It was no less an authority than Enrico Caruso who discovered her ability. For seven years she abandoned the stage and studied voice. Caruso—it was claimed—planned to sing *Manon* with l'Aguglia when she was ready—then, abruptly, he died. Mimi gave up her budding operatic career and returned to her first love—the stage. The song of the swan was heard in March 1929 at the Brooklyn Academy of Music where Mimi Aguglia sang *Carmen*.

Her travels in Spain and South America continued. But eventually she arrived in Hollywood where, along with other foreign artists, she was engaged for synchronization. In 1933 her work there was terminated, and she decided to re-visit San Francisco. People of influence in the Italian colony (such as Ettore Patrizi, editor of the newspaper *L'Italia*, and Parini, the Italian Minister of Foreign Affairs then visiting in San Francisco), urged her to produce Italian plays here.

It had been almost a decade since Mimi Aguglia had been in San Francisco. When she returned to North Beach many things had changed; among others, she had grown almost ten years older and to many the great Aguglia of the past was unknown. But time had not completely exhausted her resources nor her vigor; and in Washington Square the animated social life that radiated eagerly from the packed park benches had remained approximately the same.

L'Aguglia inaugurated her season of 1933 at the Milano Theatre in the heart of North Beach, at Washington Square and Powell. She was supported by both *L'Italia* and the local section of the Dante Alighieri Society.

As the chief representative of the Italian theatre in America, Mimi Aguglia's return could be called a triumphant one. On Tuesday, March 23, 1933, she appeared in the heart of the Italian Quarter, in an Italian theatre, the Milano (formerly the Washington Square Theatre), sponsored by the Dante Alighieri Society, the vigilant guardian of Italian culture abroad, in "an evening of Italian art."

But the vehicle selected by l'Aguglia for this important occasion was that *"sensazionale dramma,"* that classic tear-jerker, *Madame X*, by Alexander Bisson, a Frenchman!

There is no denying that *Madame X* had been one of Mimi Aguglia's most striking triumphs both on the European continent and in Latin America; that it is one of the most familiar and most sentimental dramas of modern times, the war horse of every emotional actress of every nationality, running the gamut of all the theatrical emotions, with special stress on mother love; that it has been popular in all languages, and has been adapted to the cinema innumerable times. However, for the unique occasion of a *serata d'Arte e d'Italianità* something more artistic or even more "Italian" might have been chosen.

After the heavy emotionalism of *Madame X*, a short one-act comedy, *Colei Che si Deve Amare* (*The One You Must Love*) by a San Franciscan, Paolo Pallavicini, was given, demonstrating to the satisfaction of all that Mimi Aguglia could also overwhelm the public with the *"briosissiima elettrizzante interpretazione dello scherzo."* Although the cast of *Madame X* was an unusually large one, comprising sixteen players, the one-act comedy had a cast of only four. They were:

       Minnie—Mimi Aguglia
       Marcella—Argentina Ferraù
       Alfredo—Primo Brunetti
       Aldo—Vladimiro Brunetti

With the director, Vincenzo Ferraù, these formed the nucleus of the company. Argentina Ferraù, like her mother Mimi Aguglia, started her career in the theatre very early and was a smooth and capable performer. In the next play, *Zaza*, Argentina had to play the role of a very old woman, the mother of her own mother—a difficult feat which she acquitted nobly.

For *Zaza*, performed on September 29th, tickets sold at $1.00, 75 cents, 50 cents, and 30 cents—a slight advance on the prices for *Madame X* (75 cents, 50 cents, 25 cents), but not enough to intimidate the ardent theatregoers. *Zaza*, by Berton and Simon, is another of those sentimental dramas that are especially devised to set off the emotional brilliance of Latin actresses. Playing the pathetic heroine who, from *cabotine* to star, remains *"una donna che ama e che soffre,"* Mimi Aguglia was declared to have made "audiences everywhere laugh and weep." When she gave the play in the theatre of Garbriello Rèjane in Paris, her interpretation was rated higher even than that of the French actress. Another great success for her *Zaza* was in the Broadway Theatre in New York.

So it was to Washington Square that Mimi Aguglia returned in 1933, and it was as if time had stood still; she still played in *La Cena della Beffe*, in *Fèdora*, and in *Il Padrone delle Ferriere*. The public's reception was so encouraging that she played another season during 1934-1935, this time under the sponsorship of the Italy-America Society and the Cenacolo Club.

10. THE AGUGLIA REPERTOIRE

In reviewing *Zaza*, *L'Italia* added nothing to the praises chanted after Mimi Aguglia's earlier successes in the role. Of Primo Brunetti, the leading man, it said that he acted in a dignified and distinguished manner, that he was *"ottimo e corretto sempre signore sulla scena."* It commented on the youth and intelligence of Argentina Ferraù, which were both superlative; it found something particularly nice to say about every member of the large cast.

Mimi Aguglia had given *Salomé* in English at the Greek Theatre in Berkeley, and at the Columbia Theatre; now she repeated one of her former Italian successes in San Francisco. On Wednesday, October 25th, she played again in Benelli's blank verse tragedy *La Cena delle Beffe*. She had returned to the Italian repertoire for this particular performance, for the occasion was in honor of her celebrated compatriot, Marconi, then visiting San Francisco.

On Wednesday, November 22nd, the Italian company was again borrowing from the French, playing in *La Presidentessa*, the Parisian comedy of Hennquin and Weber, a sparkling satire on the French magistrature. The success of Aguglia as the clever little Parisian actress, Gobette, was cited as proof of her versatility and competence in comedy as well as in tragedy.

Friday, December 15, was an evening of intense and profound emotion at the Milano. The provocation was the Italian drama by Camoletti, *Suor Teresa* (*Sister Theresa*), which besides the usual quota of mother love, with its sacrifices and renunciations, had the additional theme of religious exaltation. *L'Italia* commented on the eyes and the facial expression of L'Aguglia, which evoked all the anguish of the *mater dolorosa*.

In the usual paragraph devoted to costumes and stagecraft, the paper admired the *mise-en-scène*—supplied by Universal Studios—es-pecially in the scene where the nun takes her vows. It found the lighting effects, created by A. Baccari, to be richly suggestive of the religious mood; and it stressed the profound impression created by the beautiful costumes of the nun.

For the next performance, that of Friday, February 16, 1934, *Il Padrone delle Ferriere* (*The Iron Master*), was revived. This was followed on Tuesday, March 6th, by *La Nemica*, the powerful drama of Dario Niccodemi. *La Nemica*, which had been given before in San Francisco with Amelia Bruno as the protagonist, was Mimi Aguglia's favorite play; it is again, a drama of mother love, a favorite theme, as well, of the Italian theatre.

From these domestic dramas, Mimi Aguglia turned to the more esoteric emotions. Her next play was *La Tredicesima Sedia*, which can easily be recognized as the Italian version of *The Thirteenth Chair* of Bayard Vellier. This mystery drama, still occasionally revived, had played over two years in New York and was then transported throughout Europe, being especially popular in Italy—has it not the delightful combination of *"spiritismo, mistero, delitto, superstizione, amore, passione, gelosia?"* In *The Thirteenth Chair*, Mimi Aguglia had the sinister role of Madame Lagrange, the medium, at whose seance the thirteenth member is found murdered. *La Tredicesima Sedia*, performed appropriately on Friday, April 13th, must have been an exciting novelty for the public of the Milano, perhaps faintly surfeited with warmed-over revivals of the emotional classics.

On Tuesday, May 22nd, the season at the Milano, sponsored by the newspaper *L'Italia*, "for the diffusion of Italian culture," came to an end with a performance of the French drama, Sardou's *Fèdora*.

New York summoned L'Aguglia at the conclusion of this final season. The Teatro Italiano did not collapse with her departure, however. She left behind a stable foundation comprised of such zealous artists as her daughter Argentina Ferraù and the Brunettis, father and son—a framework strong enough for any theatre. And so the work continued, steadily and quietly; a group of people devoting their time and energies to a task which had no other recompense than artistic fulfillment, and no other object than to keep the spark of Italian drama burning in this alien land—the spark which had been kindled by Goldoni, Benelli, Benedetti, d'Annunzio and Pirandello, and which had been set ablaze by Adelaide Ristori, Virginia Marini, Eleonora Duse—and by Mimi Aguglia.

Undoubtedly the influence of Mimi Aguglia on the Italian theatres of the Americas was one of the most durable accomplishments of her career. She had inspired the work of D'Annunzio in her native Italy, of Dario Niccodemi in the cultivated Italian colony of Buenos Aires, and in New York she was the presiding genius over the Teatro d'Arte. In San Francisco she created the Teatro Italiano.

11. GENESIS OF THE TEATRO ITALIANO

In beginning and closing her season with the Sardou drama, Mimi Aguglia had vividly exposed the principal defect of her repertoire. Here, with so many of the rich resources of the Italian theatre to choose from, she had contented herself with rehashed translations of French and American popular classics. She was defeating the expressed aim of her theatre, which was to create a public for the specifically Italian theatre.

"*Italianità*"—devotion to Italian language and culture—increases the longer one is away from Italy. It is an attempt to cling tenaciously to that which is rapidly slipping away, the part of one's identity that is one's nationality and race. All these years a love for the theatre of Italy had been smouldering steadily in the Italian hearts of San Francisco; suddenly, at the conclusion of Mimi Aguglia's season of 1933-34, it blazed up brightly, and the Teatro Italiano was re-born in San Francisco.

The small but ardent group which was sponsoring the Teatro Italiano had asked themselves many times, "What is the use of having an Italian theatre if not to give Italian plays—and not merely translations of popular French plays and American mystery dramas?" Of the nine plays given by Mimi Aguglia in her 1933-34 season at the Milano, only three had been of Italian origin. It was decided that henceforth the Teatro Italiano would compose its repertoire, not in order to display the virtuosity of a particular star, but to exhibit to the public the most representative and significant works of Italian genius.

12. THE TEATRO ITALIANO AT THE COMMUNITY PLAYHOUSE

The shifting of Mimi Aguglia's company to the Community Playhouse was a significant move. It indicated a willingness to separate from the Italian Quarter, and it was a direct appeal to the Italian and American elite. By abandoning the popular price range of the Milano Theatre and by offering subscriptions for the six performances comprising the 1934-35 season, the company hoped to achieve more stability and permanence.

The new scale of prices was $1.25 for orchestra seats, 75 cents for the balcony, and a special subscription rate of $6.00 for all six performances. In recognition of the stated cultural and educational aims of the organization, students of Italian would only be charged 25 cents.

The name of the "new" San Francisco institution appeared for the first time on programs dated Wednesday, December 12, 1934:

Per la diffusione della cultura Italiana
MIMI AGUGLIA
Presents IL TEATRO ITALIANO *con*
"LA CENA DELLE BEFFE"
Dramma in 4 atti di Sem Benelli

La Cena delle Beffe had been an excellent choice for the inauguration of Il Teatro Italiano. It had the double virtue of being representative of the best in modern Italian drama and it was already familiar to the public as a result of Aguglia's previous interpretation.

For the next performance, on Wednesday, January 16, 1935, another work by Dario Niccodemi was given, the pathetic *Scampolo*. The play was especially chosen in commemoration of the popular Italian dramatist, well-known in the Americas, who had died a few months previously. Mimi Aguglia's impersonation of the lively, sentimental, but ingenuous, gamin Scampolo—after her success in Benelli's tragedy of cold hatred and vengeance—is an excellent example of her broad versatility, and her ability to enter readily into the life of any character. Her facility came of long association with the theatre. Perhaps being born on the stage helped.

On Wednesday, February 13th, the Teatro Italiano gave a play by d'Annunzio in which Mimi Aguglia had not yet appeared in San Francisco—*La*

Gioconda, considered by some to be the greatest work of that Italian poet. L'Aguglia's acting could not hope to compete with the famous interpretation of La Duse, for whom the play had been written; but the role of the heroic, devoted Silvia Seltala does bring out her talent for intense, vigorous acting.

Mimi Aguglia as Madame X

13. GOLDONI AND PIRANDELLO

The Teatro Italiano next chose a play representative of another order of Italian genius; this was *La Locandiera* (*The Innkeeper*) by Carlo Goldoni, performed on Wednesday, March 20th. Goldoni wrote in the eighteenth century but his comedies are everlastingly fresh. He may rightfully be called the Molière of Italy, since his position in the Italian theatre is comparable to that of the great French humorist. The Teatro Italiano was keeping its pledges to the public; it was giving as varied an assortment of representative Italian masterpieces as was possible. The graceful, witty dialogue of this delicate eighteenth century farce was indeed the antithesis of the tortured rhetoric of d'Annunzio's gloomy tragedy. From the eighteenth century, Il Teatro Italiano now leaped to the twentieth. On Wednesday, April 17th, it gave the most widely known work of Luigi Pirandello, the Italian dramatist considered by many (including the Nobel Prize judges) to be one of the greatest contemporary world-dramatists. *Sei Personnagi in Cerca d'Autore* was a play which seemed to be written for the elite. It is a strange piece, fitting none of the standard categories, utilizing a bizarre confusion of actors and audiences, paradoxical metaphysics, and a bewildering blend of reality with illusion. This first performance—in any language—of *Six Characters in Search of an Author* was a most important art event in San Francisco theatre.

The first season of the Teatro Italiano ended gloriously on Wednesday, May 8th, with another great work by Pirandello, *L'Innesto*. This play, while also possessing a philosophical theme—suggested by its title, *The Grafting*—is less involved and abstruse than Pirandello's better-known work, more conventional in its dramatic structure, and more warmly human. It is a work of pure Sicilian drama, by a Sicilian author, and the expansive Sicilian actress did full justice to all its moods, violent and tender.

During its first season Il Teatro Italiano produced only six plays; but it had given tragedy in blank verse, sentimental comedy, psychological drama, eighteenth-century farce, twentieth-century metaphysical drama, Sicilian drama. It had given six of the world's greatest plays, of varying subjects, mood, and content. It had demonstrated successfully that there was a living Italian theatre, and it furthermore demonstrated that for a Teatro Italiano there must be, above all, Italian plays. In short, "the play's the thing."

14. THE TEATRO ITALIANO CARRIES ON

The 1936 season was late in starting. After the departure of Mimi Aguglia there was an understandable period of hesitancy, during which the fate of the new enterprise seemed dubious. But the small loyal public that had been created during its brilliant first season was clamoring for the reopening of the Teatro Italiano. Mimi Aguglia had bequeathed to San Francisco a solid, capable company. The Italy-America Society, composed mainly of Americans devoted to Italian culture, and the Genacolo Club, the cultivated elite of the Italian colony, stood sturdily behind the Teatro Italiano. But it required the initiative and persistance of a few individuals like Rino Lanzoni, secretary of the Cenacolo, and Miss Esther Rossi, of the Italy-America Society, to gather together all these disparate elements and to reorganize the Teatro Italiano, somehow filling the gap caused by the departure of its star, Mimi Aguglia.

The task was simplified by the precedent established during the first season of the Teatro Italiano. By ridding her repertoire of the purely virtuoso pieces and the borrowings from foreign theatres, by performing only in the substantial works of the classic and modern Italian playwrights, Mimi Aguglia had indicated the direction the Teatro Italiano was to follow. She had bequeathed the Teatro Italiano a talented leading lady, her daughter, Argentina Ferraù, a proficient leading man, Primo Brunetti, and a director of abundant experience, Vincenzo Ferraù.

Accordingly, the new season began on Tuesday, March 24, 1936 with a play by Pirandello, *Il Piacere dell'Onestà* (*The Pleasure of Respectability*). Pirandello was followed with Goldoni's *Il Burbero Benefico* (*The Beneficent Boor*), given on Monday, April 13th, and repeated on Tuesday, April 28th. Then on Wednesday, May 6th, another modern playwright, Guglielmo Zorzi, was produced for the first time by the Teatro Italiano. His drama *In Fondo al Cuore* (*Deep in the Heart*) was given, and was the occasion for the return of Vladimiro Brunetti to the company.

On Wednesday, May 27th, the second season closed with Luigi Chiarelli's famous *grottesco*, *La Maschera e Il Volto* (*The Mask and the Face*), derived from Pirandello's philosophic dramas and ironically representing the effort of the mediocre individual to assume a mask, a manner, a dignity which he does not actually possess.

The 1936 season was unusually short, including but four plays, but the new company had, with acrobatic versatility, leaped from Pirandello's painful paradoxes to the fresh, joyous comedy of Goldoni; from the innucuous sentimentality of Zorzi's *bourgeois* drama to the cynical *grottesco* of Chiarelli.

In presenting works by completely unknown Italian playwrights, or the relatively unfamiliar works of the more famous Italian authors, the Teatro Italiano was rigorously sticking to its agenda. It was also attracting a steady public of American students of Italian and others interested in Italian culture; it was becoming an institution supplementing the work being done in the Italian schools.

The repertoire of the next season, 1936-37, was also planned carefully to be varied and representative. The Teatro Italiano was shifted to the intimate Greenroom Playhouse (1725 Washington Street), and established a tradition of six performances a season—with an occasional extra benefit performance on the first Wednesday of the month.

15. AT THE GREENROOM PLAYHOUSE

A comedy by the prolific Venetian, Goldoni, *Gli Innamorati* (*The Lovers*), was chosen again to open the season on December 2. This gay comedy of eighteenth century youthful *amours* was followed, on January 6, by Carlo Veneziani's *L'Antenato* (*The Ancestor*), a satire on twentieth century manners.

The third production of the season, on February 3, was *Due Dozzine di Rose Scarlatte* (*Two Dozen Scarlet Roses*), a comedy by Aldo de Benedetti. Aside from other considerations, the selection of this play had a symbolic value. The Italian government had given great impetus to the theatre in Italy as an important branch of national life and had instituted *Sabati Teatrali*, special performances on Sundays by all companies, at reduced rates for the working class. *Il Duce* had decided that his presence might give a certain prestige to the institution; and his official attendance had inaugurated the *Sabati Teatrali* at the Teatro Argentina in Rome. The play selected for this special event had been *Due Dozzine di Rose Scarlatte*.

This sentimental domestic comedy, quite long and full of the most extraordinary complications and intrigues, has only four characters in its cast. They were played by Argentina Ferraù, Maria Belloni, Vladimiro Brunetti, and a new member of the company, Aurelio Ferraù. Previously, in *Gli Innamorati*, another Brunetti—Arturo—had also made his debut in the small part of the waiter. Arturo had a slightly more substantial role in the next play given by Il Teatro Italiano on March 3, Pirandello's *Ma Non è Cosa Seria* (*But it Isn't a Serious Thing*). A play of paradox and observation, it is one of the best of Pirandello's satiric studies of boardinghouse life. It was especially performed to commemorate the great Italian dramatist, who had died on December 10, 1936.

On April 7, Giuseppe Adami's three-act comedy, *Felicità Colombo*, was given. It is rather innocuous in theme, but depicts the inherent strength of the Italian people, "*la vera esperessione di sano a forte popolo Italiano.*"

So far, in apparent deference to the public demand, the fare had been devoted to rather mild comedies. On May 5, however, the season was climaxed by a play of an altogether different type, a "*fantasia tragica*" by Alberto Casella, *La Morte in Vacanza*. This fantastic play, with its tragic theme, is best known in its English adaptation as *Death Takes a Holiday*, popular on both the stage and screen. The Teatro Italiano performance was the first given in its original version in America.

The next week, Tuesday, May 11, Il Teatro Italiano gave a special performance at the Veterans' War Memorial Auditorium for the benefit of the Scuola Italiana. For this occasion they repeated *L'Antenato*.

16. AT THE GOLDEN BOUGH PLAYHOUSE

The fourth season of the Teatro Italiano in the Golden Bough Playhouse began on December 8 with the production of a comedy by Testoni, *Il Nostro Prossimo* (*Love Thy Neighbor*). This was followed by a comedy by Benedetti, *Non Ti Conosco Più* (*I Don't Know You Anymore*); a farce by Goldoni in three acts and ten scenes, *La Vedova Scaltra* (*The Clever Widow*); *I Figli del Marchese Lucera* (*The Sons of the Marquis Lucera*), a domestic comedy-drama by another member of the Pirandello school, Gherardo Gherardi. The last performances of the season were Benedetti's *L'Uomo che Sorride* (*The Man Who Smiles*), and *Il Circolo Magico* (*The Magic Circle*), a fantasy by Luigi Chiorelli.

The company for this season was enriched by the presence of Oreste Seragnoli, a splendid old character actor who had appeared for many years in the popular theatre of San Francisco. He had become the director of an Italian company which gave sporadic performances in the various clubs and halls of North Beach. His company was truly a professional undertaking, however, for Seragnoli was a man of the theatre alone and had no other calling.

But most of the company of Il Teatro Italiano were amateurs in the pure sense of the word. Their venture was a non-profit, purely artistic undertaking. They perfected themselves for the performance of one play a month; they worked tremendously hard and they got very little recompense for their work, aside from the joy of acting and the satisfaction of creating a genuine Italian theatre in San Francisco.

According to Rino Lanzoni, the *metteur-en-scène* and principal organizer of the Teatro Italiano, the lack of a permanent home was one of the main reasons the theatre could not develop a richer, longer season. A favorable locale would have been Fugazi Hall in North Beach, for instance, where it might have been possible to reconcile the two distinct elements of the Italian theatre public. But the sad reality was that the Italian residents of North Beach would not venture out of their district—nor did the elitist subscribers to the Teatro Italiano wish to be seen in North Beach. The plays' sophisticated, "literary" qualities mitigated any possibility of them being repeated for a popular audience in North Beach.

The Teatro Italiano was definitely not a theatre of the people. It was an intimate theatre, subsidized by the contributions of a few ardent devoteés of Italian language and culture, such as Professor Herbert H. Vaughn of the University of California, who, for each performance, bought ten tickets to distribute among the students attending his Italian class. The members of the Italy-America Society and the Il Cenacolo Club, even when they could not attend the performance, subscribed consistently.

Thus the Teatro Italiano, with its loyal public, seemed destined to survive a few more seasons, hoping that perhaps in time it would be able to increase its repertoire enough to satisfy the popular appetite of North Beach. Perhaps, in time, they hoped, patrons would come along and endow the district with its own theatre.

A Typical Fan Program

17. SERAGNOLI AND THE POPULAR THEATRE

The Teatro Italiano had divorced itself from the "popular" theatre of North Beach and, literally speaking, the theatre which existed by the "will of the people" was dead. There was, however, one small stream which continued to flow in the channels of the popular theatre. This was the company of Oreste Seragnoli, an Italian actor of strictly professional standing. Other actors were forced to do other work for a living and could devote only their leisure time to the theatre, but Seragnoli lived by the theatre alone. For several years he organized and gave occasional performances, but not in theatres. The Italians had lost complete control of the buildings that once housed the Italian theatre: the Washington Square Theatre became the Milano, and then a cinema house called the Palace; the Liberty became a stronghold of burlesque; the Alessandro Eden became the Green Street Playhouse, and was operated by the San Francisco Theatre Union for legitimate drama with a "proletarian" slant. Seragnoli was forced to stage his plays in clubrooms, halls and auditoriums: at the Fugazi Hall, at the Verdi Club Auditorium (Mariposa Street and Potrero Avenue), at the Scottish Rite Hall, at the Unione Sportiva. Sometimes he was forced further afield into even more remote sites, such as the Grammar School Auditorium on Grand Avenue in South San Francisco. Here on April 11, 1937, his company put on *La Zia di Carlo*, which is none other than an Italian translation of the delightful English comedy, *Charley's Aunt!* Augmenting the program were several musical numbers by the Aurora Mandolin Orchestra.

April of 1937 was a strenuous month for Seragnoli. A week before *Charley's Aunt* he was playing at the Scottish Rite Hall in the Commedia Tragicomico-Musicale, a satire in three acts by Aldo Aldi, called *Il Negus alla Lega delle Nazioni*. This farce, which ridicules the League of Nations and the once-Emperor Haile Selassie, was a rather spectacular production. Seragnoli, the very proficient character actor and master of make-up, played the Negus Selassie, and Irene Veneroni, an importation from Hollywood, was L'Italia. In the large cast, which represented the various nations, officials, diplomats, etc., were, among others, Mario Scarpa (as John Bull), Joe Locatelli, Aurelio Ferraù, Arturo Brunetti, two Piccininis, two Duccinis, and a few Tricolis; there was a ballet number with twelve ballerinas, hordes of extras, and the Aurora Mandolin Orchestra.

The Aurora Mandolin Orchestra seems to be an inseparable concomitant of a Seragnoli production. A performance on May 22, 1938, also at the Scottish Rite Hall, and with the Aurora Mandolin Orchestra, was a new three-act work by Bellotti, *Il Figlio del Peccato (The Son of Sin)*.

For a time Seragnoli had to depend on the various clubs to support him, to fill his houses. He played principally for benefits. But eventually the Compagnia

Comico-Drammatica Italiana Oreste Seragnoli became a stable institution with a loyal public for its performances at the Scottish Rite or the Fugazi Hall auditoriums. The Teatro Italiano was an enterprise for the elite; but the Compagnia Seragnoli was an extrapolation of the popular theatre, such as was left of it, in San Francisco. Its efforts were directed at the great number of Italians in North Beach, and not at all at the culture-loving Americans. The *caratterista*, Seragnoli, was a genuine actor of the Italian theatre—he spoke no English.

The Compagnia Seragnoli was quite small, composed of the *capo comico* himself and a few amateurs, such as Joe Locatelli, Silvia Lenzi, Maria Piccinini, and Cosetta Cattaneo. They could not afford elaborate spectacles, and, like the Teatro Italiano, generally put on those dramas, usually comedies, which had only a few characters and required simple settings. Typical dramas were Pilotto's three-act *Il Buon Cappellano* (*The Good Chaplain*), given in September 1937 at the Verdi Club Auditorium, and Bini's *La Balia per Forza* (*The Nurse Despite Herself*). Occasionally there were offerings of a higher caliber, such as the modern drama, given in December 1937—Pirandello's *Le Sorprese del Divorzio* (*The Surprises of Divorce*). Here the Compagnia Seragnoli approached the literary repertoire of the Teatro Italiano.

18. CONCLUSION

There had indeed been a "schism" between the two theatres; but, in many ways, the gap between the popular theatre of Oreste Seragnoli and the Teatro Italiano of Mimi Aguglia and the Brunettis was not that wide. Often Seragnoli played with the Brunettis (for he *was*, after all, the greatest *caratterista* in San Francisco), and often members of the Teatro Italiano joined him in his endeavors. Italian actors of the era, though particularly prone to all kinds of rivalries and jealousies, were also willing to abandon them in order to work together harmoniously in the cause of their theatre—to keep the feeble flame of the Italian theatre burning a while longer.

Meanwhile, quietly, and without the fanfare of publicity, the companies played on, each season exhibiting to a select few the best examples of Italian theatre available to them. The Italian theatre was, perhaps, one of the most significant, if little known, artistic manifestations of San Francisco, a city long famed for its cosmopolitanism and culture.

NOTES

1. *Westways*, March 1938.
2. Scanland, J. M. *Overland Monthly*, April 1906.
3. Lola Montez. Stage name of Marie Dolores Eliza Rosanna Gilbert 1818?-1861. British dancer and adventuress. She was the mistress of Louis I of Bavaria, and under his auspices she literally controlled the Bavarian government. She captivated stage audiences in the United States and Australia during the 1850s, and eventually settled in New York where she devoted herself to the cause of helping fallen women. Author of *The Art of Beauty*.
4. Adah Bertha Menken, known as Adah Isaacs. 1835?-1868. American actress. Became the central figure in a bizarre divorce scandel. Successful on the stage, especially in *Mazeppa*. Her poetry was collected and published in 1868 under the title, *Infelicia*.
5. *Westways*, March 1938.
6. Source: Interview with Argentina Ferraù.
7. *San Francisco Chronicle*, March 2, 1924.
8. *San Francisco Chronicle*, March 11, 1924.
9. *L'Italia*, July 19, 1914.
10. *San Francisco Chronicle*, March 2, 1924.
11. *San Francisco Chronicle*, March 14, 1924.
12. *San Francisco Chronicle*, March 11, 1924.

BIBLIOGRAPHY

Ducharatre, Pierre Louis. *The Italian Comedy.* (New York: John Day Company, 1929).
Encyclopoedia Italiana, Article on "Stenterello." (San Francisco: Public Library)

NEWSPAPERS AND PERIODICALS

American Mercury. (New York), Oct. 1927. Article "Eviva San Francisco," by Idwal Jones.
Chronicle. (San Francisco), July 12, 19, 1914; March 2-17, 1924.
Corriere d'America. (Wakley, London Critic), May 21, 1935.
Il Giornale Italiano. (New York).
Il Secolo di Milano. (Italy), New York correspondent, Luigi Lucatelli.
L'Italia. (San Francisco), July 14, 19, 1914; March 2, Aug. 29, 1918; March 1919; June 1924; September, December, 1933; May 1934.
Overland Monthly. (San Francisco), April 1906. Article "An Italian Quarterly Mosaic," by J. M. Scanland.
Picayune. (San Francisco), Sept. 12, 13, 17, 24, 1850.
Westways. (Los Angeles), March 1938. Article "Episodes in Bohemia—Funicalì-Funiculà," by Idwal Jones.

APPENDIX I
MIMI AGUGLIA

Repertoire of the 1914 Season

At the Cort Theatre

July

Monday, 13	*La Figlia di Jorio* (D'Annunzio)
Tuesday, 14	*Fédora* (Sardou)
Wednesday, 15	*La Figlia di Jorio* [Matinee] (D'annunzio)
	Odette [Evening] (Sardou)
Thursday, 16	*La Cena delle Beffe* (Benelli)
Friday, 17	*La Signora delle Camelie* (Dumas)
Saturday, 18	*Malia* (Capuana)
Sunday, 19	*La Signora delle Camelie* [Matinee] (Dumas)
	La Fiaccola sotto il Moggio [Evening] (D'Annunzio)
Monday, 20	*Magda* (Sudermann)
Tuesday, 21	*Il Ladro* (Bernstein)
Wednesday, 22	*Magda* [Matinee] (Sudermann)
	Ferro [Evening] (D'Annunzio)
Thursday, 23	*Salomé* (Wilde)
	Cavallerizza
Friday, 24	*Una Americana a Parigi* (Croisset & Waliffe)
Saturday, 25	*Salomé* [Matinee] (Wilde)
	Cavallerizza
	Il Padrone delle Ferriere [Evening] (Ohnet)

AT THE WASHINGTON SQUARE THEATRE

August

Saturday, 3	*Maria Antonietta* (Giacometti)
Sunday, 4	*Madame Sans-Gêne* (Sardou)
Monday, 5	*Santorello* (Scarpetto)
Tuesday, 6	*Tosca* (Sardou)

Wednesday, 7   *Messalina* (Pietro Corda)
Thursday, 8   *Francesca da Rimini* (D'Annunzio)
Friday, 9   *Madame Sans-Gêne* [Matinee] (Sardou)
     L'Amore dei Tre Re [Evening] (Montemezzi)

REPERTOIRE OF THE 1933-34 SEASON

At The Milano Theatre

Tuesday, Mar. 23   *Madame X* (Bisson)
     Colei Che Si Deve Amare (Pallavicini)
Friday, Sept. 29   *Zaza* (Berton & Simon)
Wednesday, Oct. 25   *La Cena delle Beffe* (Benelli)
Wednesday, Nov. 22   *La Presidentessa* (Hennequin & Weber)
Friday, Dec. 15   *Suor Teresa* (Camoletti)
Friday, Feb. 16   *Il Padrone delle Ferriere* (Ohnet)
Friday, Apr. 13   *La Tredicesima Sedia* (Vellier)
Tuesday, May 22   *Fédora* (Sardou)

APPENDIX II
REPERTOIRE OF THE TEATRO ITALIANO

First Season (1934-35)
at the Community Playhouse

December 12	*La Cena delle Beffe* (Benelli)
January 5	*Scampolo* (Niccodemi)
February 13	*La Gioconda* (D'Annunzio)
March 20	*La Locandiera* (Goldoni)
April 17	*Se Personnagi in Cerca d'Autore* (Pirandello)
May 8	*L'Innesto* (Pirandello)

Second Season (1935-36)
at the Community Playhouse

March 24	*Il Piacere dell'Onesta* (Pirandello)
April 13	*Il Burbero Benefico* (Goldoni)
April 28	*Il Burbero Benefico* (Goldoni)
May 6	*In Fondo Al Cuore* (Zorzi)
May 27	*La Maschera e Il Volto* (Chiarelli)

Third Season (1936-37)
at the Green Street Theatre

December 2	*Gli Innamorati* (Goldoni)
January 6	*L'Antenato* (Veneziani)
February 3	*Due Dozzine di Rose Scarlatti* (Benedetti)
March 3	*Ma Non è Cosa Seria* (Pirandello)
April 7	*Felicità Colombo* (Adami)
May 5	*La Morte in Vacanza* (Casella)
May 11	*L'Antenata* (special benefit performance in War Memorial Auditorium per la scualo Italiana)

Fourth Season (1937-38)
at the Golden Bough Playhouse

December 8	*Il Nostro Prossimo* (Testoni)
January 5	*Non Ti Conosco Più* (Benedetti)
January 22	*Il Nostro Prossimo* (special performance at the Casa degl'Italiani (678 Green Street) for benefit of the Doposcuola G. Martini)
February 2	*La Vedova Scaltra* (Goldoni)
March 2	*I Figli del Marchesa Lucera* (Ghirardi)
April 6	*L'Uoma Che Sorride* (Benedetti)
May 5	*Il Cerco Magico* (Chiarelli)

INDEX

ACTRESSES

Aguglia, Mimi, 4, 6, 8, 11, 12, 37, 47, 73, 77-89, 91-96, 97 (portrait), 99, 106, 109
Alessandro, Antonietta (Pisanelli), 5, 7, 14 (portrait), 19-21, 30-32, 37, 41, 48-49, 66-69, 73
Aratoli, Ida, 50-51, 63
Belloni, Maria, 101
Bernardini, Regina, 12, 49, 73
Brunetta, Camilla, 50
Brunetti, Amelia, 52
Bruno, Amelia, 12, 60, 63, 93
Bruno, Stella, 70-71
Campbell, Nona (guest), 68
Campbell, Mrs. Patrick, 86
Canova, Signorita, 15
Caranza, Signora, 66
Cattaneo, Cosetta, 105
Cecchini-Aguglia, Teresa, 68
Corta, Eleana, 26
Cunico, Ester, 42, 47
Dosseno, Adelina, 40
Duccinis, The, 104
Duse, Eleanora (guest), 12, 78, 84-86, 88-91, 94-97
De Matienzo, Teresa, 3, 49
Di Lorenzo, Tina, 77, 85
Di Grazia, Signora, 26
Ferraù, Argentina, 7, 53, 77, 92-94, 99, 101, 107, 120 (portrait)
Garuffi, Maria, 70
Illington, Margaret, 86
Lenzi, Silvia, 105
Maori, Concetta, 42-43, 45, 65
Maori, Maria, 42
Manten, Fannie, 15
Marini, Virginia, 94
Miceli, Maria, 68
Modotti, Tina, 4, 8, 52, 60-62, 120 (portrait)

Modjeska, 86
Montez, Lola, 62, 107
Minciotti, Ester
Minciotti, Ernestina
Menken, Adah Isaacs, 62, 107
Palange, Signora, 48
Parisi, Signora, 68
Piccinini, Maria
Pisanelli, Antonietta, *see* Alessandro, Antionetta
Réjane, Garbriello, 84, 92
Ringo, Florence (guest), 68
Ristori, Adelaide, 78, 94
Rondera, Signora, 49
Rossi, Esther, 8, 99
Tetrazzini, Luisa, 17
Todini, Santuzza, 69
Tricoli, Lidia (child), 53
Veneroni, Irene (guest), 104
Vittorina, 50

ACTORS AND IMPRESARIOS

Aguglia, Gigi, 68, 73
Alessandro (child), 31
Aratoli, Alfredo, 3, 12, 37, 38 (portrait), 49-52, 54-55, 60, 69-71
Badolati, Luigi, 70-71
Brunetti, Arturo, 101, 104
Brunetti, Primo, 7, 12, 73, 77, 92-93, 99
Brunetti, Vladimiro, 7, 77, 92, 99, 101, 120 (portrait)
Cacciarelli, A., 49
Cecchini, Signor, 68
Cecchini, Totò (child), 68
Del Buono, Luigi, 35
De Cesare, Francesco, 33
Di Grazia, Signor, 26
Duccinis, The, 104
Ferraù, Aurelio, 101, 104
Ferraù, Vencenzo, 11, 77, 82, 92, 99
Ferrier, André, 77-78
The Francos, 42
Godi, Arturo, 33, 35, 38 (portrait), 40
Gravina, Cesare, 63
Grillo, Antonio, 50
Lanzoni, Rino, 7, 99, 102
Locatelli, Joe, 104-105

Luigi, Signor, 18
Macagno, G., 18
Magagna, Ismael, 63-64
Maori, Antonio, 21, 41-45, 47, 65
Mariotti, Adolfo, 40
Martinelli, Enrico, 68-69
Mattioli, Gigi, 52, 60
Mezzacapo, S., 49
Migliaccio, Edoardo, 55-58, 60
Miceli, Giuseppe, 69
Minciotti, Silvio, 4
Parisi, Signor, 68
Poggi, Luigi, 63
Porreca, Camillo, 8, 64-65
Pinto (family), 42
Puglia, Frank, 37, 63, 73
Roose, 50
Rossi, 11, 15, 17
Scarpa, Mario, 8, 12, 32, 40, 42-43, 47, 49, 51, 60, 71, 73, 104
Schipa, Tito (guest), 68
Seragnoli, Oreste, 8, 47, 52, 63, 102, 104-106
Serantoni, August, 37, 65
Suar, 15
Sterni, 84, 86
Salvini, Gustavo, 43, 79
Todini, Renzo, 69
Trento, Guido, 68-69
Tricoli, Carlo, 3, 5, 8, 49, 51-53, 60, 63, 71, 76 (portrait), 104
Tirado, Romualdo, 66

THEATRES, HALLS, PLAYHOUSES

Alessandro Eden Theatre, 4, 12, 67-70, 72-73, 104
Apollo Hall (Teatro Apollo), 3, 11, 18-19, 21, 73
Beach Theatre, 32
Bersaglieri Hall, 21
Bijou Theatre, 11, 32-33, 35
California Theatre, 48
Circolo Famigliare Pisanelli, 3, 11, 22-23, 26-30, 33, 67
Columbia Theatre, 93
Community Playhouse, 4, 12, 96, 111
Cort Theatre, 11, 47, 84-87, 109
Crescent Theatre, 66
Fugazi Hall, 102, 104-105
Giambelli Hall, 19

Golden Bough Playhouse, 4, 12, 37, 102, 112
Grammar School Auditorium, 104
Greek Theatre, UC Berkeley, 93
Green Street Theatre, 67, 104, 111
Greenroom Playhouse, (Group met later at the Fairmont Hotel, San Francisco), 4, 12, 100-101
Iris, 11, 32
Liberty Theatre, 3, 12 48-50, 52-54, 58, 60, 66, 71-72, 104
Milano Theatre (Teatro Milano), 12, 37, 53, 73, 91, 93-96, 104, 110
Palace, 37, 104
Scottish Rite Hall, 104-105
Silesian Auditorium, 51
Teatro Italiana di Varietà: see Alessandro Eden
Unione Sportiva, 53, 104
Verdi Club Auditorium, 104-105
Veterans' War Memorial Auditorium, 101
Washington Square Theatre, 3, 11-12, 37-38, 41, 43, 45, 47-48, 51-52, 60, 62-63, 65, 71-73, 87-88, 91, 104, 109

COMPANIES AND TROUPES

Aguglia Troupe, 8, 47, 88, 92, 96, 99
Bruno-Seragnoli Company, 12, 60, 62
Cesare Company, 11, 21, 33, 40-41
Circolo Famigliare Pisanelli, 30
City of Florence Company, 49, 70
Compagnia Città di Firenze, 12, 50, 60, 70-71
Compagnia Comica-Drammatica Italiana, 11, 37
Compagnia Comica-Drammatica Italiano Oreste Seragnoli, 104-105
Compagnia dei Sette, 68, 73
Compagnia Drammatica Aratoli, 52
Compagnia Italiana de Mationzo, 48, 52
Latin Quarter Opera Company, 12, 63
Maori Company, 3, 11, 37, 41-47, 71-76
Minciotti Company, 12, 42, 71
La Moderna Comic Opera Company, 12, 63
La Moderna Grand Opera Company, 12, 63
Puglia Company, 12
Rapone Company, 11, 21, 30
Società Fraterna, 19

PLAYS AND OPERAS

Acqua Chieta (operetta), 70
Addio Giovanezza (operetta), 70

Aïda (opera), 63
Une Américaine à Paris, 87
L'Ammore dei Tre Re, 88, 110
Amleto (Hamlet), 43, 45
L'Antenato, 101, 111
Avvocato e il Pizzi-Cagnolo, 45
La Balia, 40
La Balia per Forza, 105
The Barber of Seville, 46
Beppe Melacine, 72
Il Biricchino di Parigi, 72
The Bohemian Girl, 24, 28
Il Buon Cappelano, 105
Burbero Benefico, 99, 111
Caino e Abele, 40
Il Cappriccioi di un Padre, 40
La Casa del Peccato, 53
Casa Paterna (Magda), 45
Casta Susanna, 69
La Cavolaia di Firenze, 50
Cavalleria Rusticana 18, 20, 31, 73
Cavallerizza, 87, 109
La Cena delle Beffe, 52, 85, 93, 96, 109-111
The Chaste Susanna (operetta), 70
Il Circolo Magico, 102, 112
La Città Morta, 89
Colei Che si Deve Amare, 92, 110
Così Sia, 90
The Count of Luxembourg (operetta), 70
The Count of Monte Cristo, 71
Dall'Ombre al Sole, 60
Il Deputato de Bombignac, 45
Il Duca Giardiniere (operetta), 72
La Duchesse du Bal Tabarin, 63
Due Dozzine di Rose Scarlatti, 101, 111
Le Due Orfanelle, 40
L'Elisir d'Amore (opera), 63
Er Fatacio, 72
Faust, 45
La Favorite, 63
Fèdora, 71, 84, 92, 94
Felicità Colombo, 101, 111
Ferro, 86, 109
La Fiaccola Sotto il Moggio, 85, 109
La Figlia della Strada, 72

I Figli del Marchese Lucera, 102, 112
Il Figlio del Peccato, 104
La Figlia di Jorio, 81, 83-85, 109
Fra Diavolo (opera), 63
Francesca da Rimini, 71, 88, 110
La Fucilazione di Pulcinella, 39
La Gioconda, 97, 111
Gianciotto, 69
Here Comes the Bride, 53
His Majesty the Dollar, 70
Illusi, 69
L'Incontro di Pasquariello e Stenterello, Tormentati dall'Araticolo 139, 39
In Fondo al Cuore, 99, 111
Gli Innamorati, 101, 111
L'Innesto, 98, 111
Kean Ovvero Genio e Sregolatezza, 41
Il Ladro, 86, 109
Il Lampionario de Porto, 39
La Locandiera, 98, 111
Lucia di Lammermoor (opera), 28
La Lupa del Mare, 32
Madama 4 Soldi, 45
Madame Sans-Gêne, 88, 109-110
Madame X, 92, 110
Malia, 80, 85, 109
Ma Non è Cosa Seria, 101, 111
Maria Antonietta, 88, 109
Marinaio per Forza ed Uccisor di Briganti, 70
La Maschera e il Volto, 99, 111
The Merchant of Venice, 43
Messalina, 88, 110
Il Misteri dell'Inquisizione di Spagna, 45
La Monaca Bianca, 71
La Monaca di Cracovia, 45
La Morte Civile, 52, 60, 71-72
La Morte e Passione di N.S. Gesu' Cristo, 50
La Morte in Vacanza, 101, 111
Il Negus alla Lega delle Nazioni, 104
La Nemica, 52, 60, 73, 93
Non Ti Conosco Più, 102, 112
Il Nostro Prossimo, 102, 112
Una Notte a Firenze, 45
Nu Guaglione è Malavita, 66
Odette, 85, 109
Otello (Othello), 28, 43, 45, 50, 53, 71, 79

Il Padrone delle Ferriere, 87, 92-93, 109-110
I Pagliacci, 63
Pasquariello Madre Senze Figli e Zia Senz Nipoti, 39
La Petite Chocolatière, 70
Il Piccolo Demonietto, 68
Piedigrotta 1925, 72
Il Piacere dell' Onesta, 99, 111
La Porta Chiusa, 89
La Presidentessa, 93, 110
Il Ratto delle Savine, 45
Rigoletto (opera), 24, 28, 63
La Rivoluzione Russ, 60
Romanticismo, 45
Il Romanzo d'un Farmacista Povero, 45
Giulietta e Romeo (Romeo and Juliet), 43, 45, 71
Santorella, 88
Scampolo, 60, 62, 96, 111
Salomé, 83, 86-87, 93, 109
Scarpetta, 49
Sei Personnagi in Cerca d'Autore, 98
La Signora delle Camelie, 40, 45, 85, 109
The Slipper Lost in the Snow, 70
La Societa Tromboni, Bombardini e Corni, 70
Le Sorprese del Divorzio, 105
Spettri, Gli (Ghosts), 52, 60, 89
Stenterello, Fruttivendolo e Salvatore della Patria, 39
Stenterello Servitore de Quattro Padroni, 39
Suor Teresa, 93, 110
The Taming of the Shrew, 43
La Tigre di Bengala, 40
La Tosca, 49, 60, 71, 88, 109
La Traviata (opera), 28, 63
La Tredicesima Sedia, 93-94, 110
I Tre Moschetieri, 71
The Two Orphans, 40, 45
L'Uomo che Sorride, 102
La Vedova Allegra, 63
La Vedova Scaltra, 102, 112
Veneranda Porto, Ovvero il Delitto di Tommaso Centenari, 70
The Victim of Tevere, 70
Zaza, 92-93, 110
La Zia di Carlo, 104

Three Leading Actors of the Italian Theatre

Vladimiro Brunetti—Argentina Ferraù—Tina Modotti

www.ingramcontent.com/pod-product-compliance
Lightning Source LLC
LaVergne TN
LVHW041630070426
835507LV00008B/547